CHRISTENA ESTBY

Greater Than Grief:
Two Brothers Against Duchenne

First published by Independently Published 2022

First edition

ISBN: 979-8-36-092655-9

This book was professionally typeset on Reedsy.
Find out more at reedsy.com

~For my family~
Cory - I appreciate your support and companionship more than you know. Your even temperament and diplomatic touch bring just the right balance to our household.

Gabriel & Kaleigh (aka the big kids) - In many ways you've made parenting easier than it could have been, while teaching me priceless lessons along the way. I am so very proud of the young adults you've become.

Samuel & Josiah - You inspire me every day to learn, to advocate, and to love more fiercely.
~Love you all~

Contents

Foreword

I have had the honor of calling Christena my friend for over 35 years—what a gift that friendship has been to me! And what a gift this book will be to you, because as you read *Greater than Grief*, you will feel invited into the life of the Estby family to share in their fabulous chaos, laughter, antics, tears, discovery, learning, and the deep-rooted faith that binds them together as they embark on this journey through life with a terminal diagnosis.

When Christena first posed the question looking for someone interested in running the 2020 Chicago Marathon with her, it was a no-brainer for me to say yes. I understood that it would be an incredible challenge, but I looked forward to the training alongside (virtually, as we live in different states) and running on race day with Christena. Truth be told, part of my reason to say yes was good-old fear of missing out (if I were younger and cooler, would I have said FOMO?).

Her transparency with struggles and purity of joy in our successes kept me encouraged and inspired to keep putting one tired foot in front of the next, month after month! As I prepped for race day, it occurred to me that training for the race was just like our years of friendship: There is no missing out when you are friends with someone who embraces life the way Christena does.

In this book, she has written her family's beautiful story, yet you will see how it is God who has masterfully crafted these characters and storyline: the chapters already known and those yet to be discovered by the Estby family. Christena's love for her family, her heart's desire to provide the best life possible for her boys, and her passion to educate those around her while also being a support to others who are navigating a Duchenne diagnosis are reflective of our heavenly Father's love for us.

Christena plays many roles in her life and with this, her debut book, she can add gifted author to that list. It is my great pleasure to introduce to you my dear friend, Christena Estby.

-Anne L. Benson

See how great a love the Father has bestowed upon us,
that we would be called children of God: and such we are.
I John 3:1 (The Message)

Preface

I love words. I always have. I toyed with the idea of writing for quite some time before actually putting fingertips to keyboard. I really didn't think I had anything worthy enough to record for posterity. I doubted I had much of a story to tell, or that anyone would care about the things I think are noteworthy or important. I find our life experiences and family make-up to be fascinating, but then again, it's MY family and OUR experience. Maybe that sounds pretty egotistical. Does it? Who else would even have an interest?

After several conversations with friends and encouragement to think about the uniqueness of our family's story, while at the same time considering how relatable it might be to others, here I am, writing a book. If nothing else, I hope this will be some really good therapy for me throughout the writing process.

Our family's journey touches on pregnancy loss, the stress of a NICU stay and resulting permanent hearing loss, foster care/adoption, a rare disease diagnosis, parenting, homeschooling, faith…so many topics that are a touchpoint in some way or another for others. I hope that by writing about many of these experiences and feelings over the last several years I can bring a clarity to those memories for myself and move to the forefront a reminder of God's faithfulness to us always.

We've had quite a journey so far, with hardships, tears, and frustrations. There have been so many wonderful experiences and countless joys as well. We are immeasurably blessed by the group of people surrounding us, sharing incredible love, compassion, and kindness with our family. God's plan has been revealed to us in bits and pieces, certainly not always in our time, but His. Through seasons of struggle, we cling to our faith, seeking guidance and peace.

Knowing that your loved one has a terminal diagnosis changes so many things. How do you successfully navigate through the day-to-day of life when this knowledge is always lurking in the background? Do you cry and scream and grieve? Do you research and fundraise and fight? Do you do both?

How do you interact with friends, family, and the stranger on the street? How do you engage with those who can't possibly understand what you're experiencing emotionally, physically, mentally, and spiritually? How do you educate and advocate with grace, peace, poise, and confidence? How do you love that loved one—embracing moments and experiencing joys—despite the sadness continually resting on your spirit?

Anticipatory grief (the feeling of grief occurring before an impending loss) is very real, and it certainly is nothing unique to me and my family. The length of time for this process can vary greatly—How long does the particular decline last (months or years)? What level of additional support (nursing care, medical devices, or transportation assistance) do you have? What is your relationship with the affected person (spouse, parent, or child)? What coping skills and aids do you have in place?

Two people I love with all my being have Duchenne Muscular

Dystrophy, and in spite of all of our efforts (physical therapy, quality medical care, healthy diet, clinical trials, medication and supplements, and all the love in the world), barring an actual, honest to goodness direct-from-God miracle, Duchenne will kill them. It will rob them of so much BEFORE then, but in the end, complications from the thief named Duchenne will take them from us entirely too soon.

I aim to look to the future with hope, fully aware that this unending underlying sadness will be my companion. I want to continue to process and envision what Duchenne holds for my sons' futures, being realistic and as prepared as we can for those changes when they come. At the same time, I go on making memories with my family, doing my best to live in the moment, and loving these boys fiercely. We offer opportunities for education, and we learn right alongside them. We aim to discover those things they want to do over and over again. We hope to fill their lives and ours with a spirit of peace and contentment while looking forward to new and exciting experiences. I pray daily for peace in my heart, a continued trust in God, and an appreciation for those who are journeying beside us offering prayer, conversation, and support.

There is no cure. There is no fix. Many times I don't feel there is much I can do other than stand by and wait for those future changes to arrive. However, I do have a voice. I have a story to tell and experiences to share. I can help others learn more about Duchenne through our sons' lives and our family's journey.

Maybe these words can bring someone else comfort, knowing that this type of loss and grief is shared, if even in different circumstances from our own. Despite the sadness, there can be a sense of peace in knowing you're not alone in what you're living and feeling. Everyone has a story, unique and profound. We all have our share of grief and joy, and we look for hope amid trials. We all need support, love, and a bit of extra care at some point in our lives. I have come to truly believe that we, as humans, are so much more alike than we are different despite backgrounds, upbringings, and belief systems. We all participate in the human experience, and with that comes the highest of highs and the lowest of lows, navigating relationships and living life together.

I pray that our family's story will be a blessing to you.

Acknowledgement

Writing a book is no small task. I had the encouragement from others to tell our family's story, but that also meant I would have to be completely open and *vulnerable.* Being that unguarded has never been my natural inclination. However, once I started replaying memories, formulating an overall layout, and actually began typing, I felt an urgency to get this story told. I hope *Greater Than Grief: Two Brothers Against Duchenne* finds its intended audience: families handed a Duchenne diagnosis, other medical and special needs moms and dads, adoptive families, Christian parents, and anyone who simply finds some connection between our story and their own.

The time invested in the actual writing of a manuscript pales in comparison to the time spent preparing it to be published. I owe a huge debt of thanks to the special people who served as pre-readers, editors, and encouragers: Anne, Kim, Barb, Tara, Pat, Constance, Lauren, Barbara, and Karen. Your time is valuable, and I greatly appreciate your willingness to help me with this crucial task.

Thank you to the Estby brood (Cory, Gabriel, Kaleigh, Samuel, and Josiah) for your support. Even though I had the writing mostly completed before you even knew this idea existed, you have participated in this journey and inspired most of what I've written. Thank you for your continued support as I figured out the "next steps" to getting this story published.

One

Begin at the Beginning

I t all started with a phone call in the Kohl's parking lot.

"Hi, it's Leah. I know you've been hoping to adopt for quite some time now and didn't know if you would even be interested, but my friend was just telling me about a 7-week-old little boy they're calling Oscar. They are looking for a family to adopt him. He has been diagnosed with Duchenne Muscular Dystrophy. I don't necessarily know what that means for the long-term, but I can give you the agency info if you like."

Duchenne? Nope, I didn't know what that was. I had a very vague awareness of muscular dystrophy in general. Vague, meaning I used to watch the Jerry Lewis Telethon on Labor Day weekend with my family most years. I knew that "Jerry's Kids" had muscular dystrophy. That was truthfully the extent of my knowledge base at that time.

A five minute phone call on a Saturday afternoon in February

(At least I think it was afternoon? Was it even a Saturday?) changed my life and the dynamic of our household permanently. Leah gave me the social service agency phone number and let us take it from there.

Those outside of the adoption world maybe don't understand the intensity and speed with which you sometimes have to respond to a phone call, text, or email. Families wishing to adopt often wait lengthy periods of time, hoping and praying an expectant mother will choose them. The money invested, in many cases, doesn't allow for opportunity to start over if something falls through. Multiple couples may be in communication with the same expectant mother. It can feel like a competition. Sadly, despite best efforts, these children sometimes seem like commodities. "We need to jump on this opportunity, RIGHT NOW!"

That mindset isn't natural for my husband and me. We like to plan, discuss, and mull over. We don't delay for a crazy amount of time in anything we do, but definitely prefer to feel a bit educated and have time for a real conversation before making a confident decision. That's not always possible in adoption, and often there are so many unknowns and *what ifs*, no matter how many questions you ask or how prepared you might feel.

Here's where a little backstory comes in. My husband, Cory, and I had been married for almost 15 years and already had two biological children (Gabriel, 11 and Kaleigh, 9) at this point. Around the time Kaleigh was 3 years old, we completed foster parent training and served in that capacity for a brief period. We then took a pause while I went back to work for awhile, finally deciding to pursue infant adoption through an agency.

We had talked about wanting to consider adoption, even before we were married, and we felt we were on the right path.

However, after four years contracted with an adoption agency and loads of money later, we had been matched with four expectant mothers resulting in four failed adoption attempts for various reasons: one expectant mother changed her mind early on in the match; one backed out after her grandparents threatened to kick her out of their house if she relinquished her parental rights; another had a stillbirth at 26 weeks; and finally, one changed her mind two days after the birth of her baby girl, deciding to parent. This was especially difficult for us, as we had traveled to Ohio to meet the baby, bonded with her over those couple of days, and fully expected to bring a new daughter home. Instead, we returned to Illinois with empty arms and broken hearts.

Here we were in February 2014, a year after that fourth adoption loss. We wondered how such a large gap in age between the kids at this point would potentially affect family dynamics. We were concerned about how much more waiting and promise and highs and lows we could each handle emotionally. We were uneasy about the debt we had already incurred and apprehensive about whether or not it would even be possible to continue.

How much more were we willing or even able to borrow? How were these emotional ups and downs really affecting our kids over all this time? How long was too long? How much was too much? We previously renewed our agency contract several times, to the tune of an additional financial commitment with each renewal. We had questioned why we were overlooked by so many birth mothers. To our knowledge, we had been presented—offered as an option—to more than 100 birth mothers total over that four year time frame.

Again, if not familiar with the adoption process: As a

prospective adoptive couple, you typically develop a profile or look-book of sorts, showing your home, your family, and support system. It's basically a sneak peak into your life. The idea is to display through a mixture of pictures and words why you would be an amazing choice to raise someone's child.

Cory and I were pretty pleased with how our profile turned out. With delay after delay, and after repeatedly not being chosen when we knew we were "in the running" with two or three other couples, we ended up asking questions. We were told it could be any number of things that may have excluded us: the fact that we already had children, as some birth mothers want to be able to give the gift of a child to a couple who otherwise wouldn't have one; the fact that Cory is a pastor could possibly lead to an expectant mother feeling judged; the fact that we live in a very rural community; even the fact that we have a dog, but not a cat. Literally anything could be the trigger for choosing or refusing a couple. Truthfully, the power lies with the birth mother. Long ago, the next couple on the list was able to adopt the next baby to become available. This is definitely not how things are done now.

We had come to the point where we were seriously weighing our options. We prayed, asking God to bring peace to our spirits and strongly considered putting an end to this roller coaster. Despite attempts to grow our family through foster care and adoption over the previous seven years, Cory and I finally came to the difficult decision to simply embrace our little family of four. The final agency contract period was to expire the following month. We would not be renewing again.

Enter this phone call. We figured the agency wouldn't be open until Monday morning anyway, so we had the weekend to do some research. We chose additional keywords to search once we learned pieces of an entirely new vocabulary related to Duchenne: dystrophin protein, prednisolone, Gower's maneuver, rhabdymyolysis, and exons. We read about progression, expected lifespan, common concurrent learning disabilities, and potential effects the lack of dystrophin has on emotional regulation and brain development. We learned about possible treatments—not many. We read about options for a cure—none. We read about prospective medications and procedures currently being studied in the lab or entering clinical trial. SO MUCH INFORMATION IN SUCH A SHORT TIME.

It was overwhelming. We had to weed through a lot of outdated information. We sought as many reputable online resources as we could in order to be able to make an educated decision about our abilities and preparedness to consider voicing interest in bringing this little boy home.

We talked and prayed and read some more. We'd been waiting so long, but this seemed so big. Too big? Truth be told, bare bones honesty—and every time I've thought about it or said it out loud, I have felt convicted—I know with all certainty that if we had been offered the opportunity to adopt a baby with such a serious medical diagnosis (a baby like Oscar) even six months earlier, our answer would have been "no."

We had said all along that we just hoped to provide a home to a child in need. That is entirely true at its core. However, we had protected ourselves from difficult or uncertain situations before. When offered a match with an expectant birth mother serving time in prison and admitting to heavy drug use, we took a pass. When presented with a situation in which the birth father was quite likely not willing to sign over his parental rights, we said "no thank you," because we weren't willing to take that chance.

It had taken that lengthy period (seven years since we had begun our foster parent training), the financial loss (approximately $25,000 up to this time), and the emotional upheaval to bring both of us—*mostly me?*—to this point. God had prepared our hearts for openness to this child and his difficult situation. We later found out that another couple had been matched for adoption with Oscar and his birth mother prior to delivery. They then backed out after learning of his diagnosis. At first thought, it would be so very easy to judge them and question their commitment. But I was them, as altruistic as I believed my motives to have been, the reality was that all along I'd hoped for, planned for, and expected a "healthy" child.

Our ridiculous journey took us from hoping to adopt a child to add to OUR family or wanting to fill a need in OUR lives, to coming across (or more accurately, having dropped in our laps) a child who truly was in need of a family and a home to call HIS own.

That phone call led to much conversation, many additional questions, wondering whether we were equipped to take this on, yet an unexpected confidence that we would figure it out.

Fast forward through the next week: a flurry of phone calls, a home visit, in-person interviews with each member of our household, and finally, the opportunity to meet Oscar. The social worker who visited with us in our home seemed thrilled we had older kids who were very independent, we were experienced parents, and by the time this baby would have serious physical and medical needs, our older two would be grown adults. In theory, when the time came, Cory and I would be able to focus our energies on our youngest.

Throughout our married life, we had already experienced our

share of sadness and loss: the stillbirth of a little girl we named Caitlyn a year before our son, Gabriel, was born; a 16-day NICU stay for Gabriel as a newborn so very sick with group B strep—later leading to a diagnosis of a moderate/severe hearing loss, likely as a side effect of the strong antibiotics that saved his life; difficult fostering experiences; and all the failed adoption attempts.

However, the moment the social worker first placed the baby (we named him Samuel, which means "God has heard") in my arms, I knew, I felt it: This baby is absolutely who God meant for us all along. His timing, not ours. This little guy is our son. We brought him home exactly one year to the day after our return home from Ohio empty handed. We settled into whatever this new normal would become. It had been so long since we'd had a baby in the house. The big kids loved their little brother immensely and our family finally felt complete.

Two

Wait, What?

Long before finding out Samuel existed, I had resigned from my position as a preschool teacher in order to be ready whenever we were to hear the good news about a baby coming to join us. Because of those several hiccups in our adoption journey, I ended up not working a regular job for the two years leading up to his arrival. I did some babysitting, taught piano lessons, occasionally played the organ for church, and served as a substitute teacher at my kids' school, in addition to hours and hours of volunteer time there.

Once Samuel was home, Cory and I had some serious discussions about household dynamics and the interactions between the kids. We were both concerned that the greater than originally expected or intended gap in age between our kids could make it exceedingly difficult for the three Estby children to have any sort of real relationship. The big two were in 6th and 4th grade, at school all day, and involved in dance, soccer, and other activities in the evenings. When would they ever actually be able to spend time together?

We started to consider the idea of homeschooling. The pros of freedom of schedule along with the ability to choose our curriculum and work at the pace best suited to the kids seemed promising. The opportunity for them to work independently to a great extent, have a shorter school day, be able to participate in Samuel's daily care and family outings, and just simply living life together seemed to far outweigh the cons, at least to the two adults in the household.

We sat Gabriel and Kaleigh down one evening and told them we'd been considering this as an option for the next school year. We talked at length about friendships, routine, and the comfort of what they've known and experienced for years. We laid out our thoughts on the positives homeschooling could offer, came up with a short list of cons together, and then asked for their opinions. They both were immediately in favor of giving it a try. We all entered with the mindset of giving it a solid effort, but knew at any time we could always choose to re-enroll them in traditional school.

Homeschooling began that August. Despite switching gears with curriculum choices a time or two and occasional bouts of laziness during which it was a struggle to get either or both of them to complete their work, we had a lot of success. Most importantly, both Gabriel and Kaleigh were, and continue to be, an active and involved part of their brother's life. They changed diapers and fed bottles. They played peekaboo and later Monopoly Jr. and UNO. They accompanied us to the park and on group Costco runs, and now they sometimes serve as chauffeurs themselves.

Like most brothers and sisters in pretty much any family, there are arguments and some yelling, name calling and bad attitudes. However, there also is clearly so much love between this group of siblings. Samuel looks up to his big brother and sister with great admiration, and the big kids are amused and amazed by his cleverness and wit, his sweet smile and goofy laugh.

We have always completed school work four days each week, allowing some freedom to skip a day if things get busy or to purposefully plan for a field trip or outing. We also basically school year-round. We take a few days off at Christmas, but definitely not two to three weeks. In the summer we might cut back to three days of school some weeks. I don't feel the need to carry a load of school books and activities with us when we're on vacation, so we don't, but there is always continual forward progress.

Throughout this process I have come to the understanding that although homeschooling is truly not a viable choice for every family, and there are some who simply have zero interest in doing so, a motivated parent can do it well. No one has your child's best interest at heart more than you do as an involved and active parent. There are supports like tutors, online programs, and co-ops if you choose to go that route. There are curriculum fairs, homeschool conventions, and Facebook groups. Everyone's homeschooling journey is unique, and although there are some certain basic standards that need to be met, there is so much flexibility. There are innumerable opportunities to try something new. Yes, it's not for everyone, but homeschooling has turned out to be a wonderful choice for our family.

But, wait! Something's missing! The story isn't complete yet.

When Samuel was about 18 months old, I had a dream. I don't remember many specifics now, but in that dream, the gist was that Samuel's birth mother was expecting another baby. I just kept thinking over and over:

"We should help."

"What happens if this baby has Duchenne too?"

"Will they have trouble finding a home for him?"

So many questions brought on by the workings of a mind whose body was supposedly at rest. The details are foggy, but the message was clear: I had strong feelings about the possibility of a sibling at some point in the same position/predicament that 7-week-old Samuel was in when we were introduced to him.

I was rattled. I never have vivid dreams. The memories and stories I imagine in my sleep so often fade away as soon as morning light arrives. I kept it to myself for a couple of days, mulling over my thoughts about the possibility, thinking (perhaps too much) about my feelings surrounding the idea of another baby, and realizing how ridiculous it seemed that I was worrying about an imaginary child. These were all what ifs, as we didn't even have any contact with Samuel's birth mother (her choice). It was just a dream. Or maybe a hunch? Or simply a wish? Was this God telling me something or were these middle of the night thoughts brought on by some deep down anxiety about our ability to manage Samuel's eventual needs?

I finally shared my thoughts with Cory, told him about my dream, and asked him what I should do about the nagging feeling in my gut. I wondered if he'd be open to the idea of maybe adopting again should the right circumstance be in front of us. He took it in stride like he takes everything in stride. He's Cory. Those who know him know that's what he does. He listened, thought for a moment, and then suggested we send an email to the agency letting them know of our potential interest if the opportunity came along.

We reached out to the agency a day or two later. Basically, we let them know that Cory and I had been discussing "on the off, off, off chance that Samuel's birth mom would ever show up and want to make another adoption plan, we hoped they would consider us first." I suppose we were asking them to offer us rights of first refusal, so to speak. The response was very appreciative and the social worker let us know the agency would definitely be in contact if Samuel's birth mother ever came to them seeking placement for another baby. She told us they had not heard from his birth mother since the surrender paperwork was signed for Samuel's adoption a year and a half prior, but she would be happy to put a copy of our email in his file to join the letter and photo updates we had already sent.

Mission accomplished. The weight was off of my heart. I could put it out of my mind because Cory and I had followed that gut feeling and gotten the info out to the people who needed to know.

Excellent. Carry on.

Cue another phone call exactly two weeks later. Cory was the one on the phone, but I could hear every word spoken. Samuel's birth mother had come into the agency's office that afternoon, seven and a half months pregnant with Samuel's full biological sibling, seeking to make an adoption plan. Wait, what? Are you kidding me? For real?

The conversation continued. Once Samuel's birth mother was there, sitting in the office, the social worker shared our email with her. She seemed a little surprised we had reached out, but she wanted to know if we would consider adopting this baby too.

While hearing the words being spoken, I made eye contact with Cory and just started silently nodding my head. You know those times in your life when you feel God is CALLING you to something? Those are the times you can't possibly do anything other than say, "yes, of course." So…we said, "yes, of course."

When an adoption is finalized (at least in our state and at that time), your family's file is closed. If you wish to adopt again, the process basically begins all over—completing a home study, gathering financial information, physical exams for everyone in the household, TB tests, retaining an adoption attorney, providing a list of all medications in the home, a well water test, proof of rabies vaccination for the dog, letters of recommendation, an interview/assessment of your emotional and psychological "fitness" to bring a child into the home, and so much more. It's A LOT. Obviously, the time required can vary more or less depending on your own speed and efficiency and the time spent waiting for appointments and requested information to be returned to you, but the paperwork process can typically take six to nine months.

We contacted the agency that had helped us complete our home study from the very beginning of the adoption journey through Samuel's homecoming. Tara, one of the social workers there, was again our partner in this process. Our paperwork for adopting Samuel's sibling took just under five weeks. It was completed four days before the baby was born.

There was such a flurry of activity as I became the Queen of All Things Documentation: filling out forms, sending emails, scheduling appointments, mailing stuff off, even including the occasional phone call—and if you know me at all, you know I don't do phone calls. Amid questions about school stuff from the big kids, daily care for Samuel's needs, and the mundane—like cleaning the house and buying groceries, I filled out some forms and saved a pile for Cory to come home to sign each evening. Our file expanded with each passing day as I ticked a few more items off of the to-do list.

We received the call on a Saturday morning that the baby, a boy, had been born. The law in our state requires 72 hours before parental rights can be signed over, so we had made arrangements for the other three kids to stay with our friends (Jeff, Angela, and their daughter, Lily) for a couple of days to allow us to meet this new little guy and await the all-clear to bring him home. Our chosen name for him was Josiah, which means "God heals." Not only did we like the way it sounded with the other kids' names: Gabriel, Kaleigh, and Samuel, we also hoped it to be an appropriate choice; offering healing for our hearts, peace for his birth family, and the like. It was a pretty short trip to go meet him. The hospital was just a little more than two hours from our home.

We made it to the hospital when Josiah was about four hours old. The labor and delivery floor was quiet at that time, as several other babies had just recently gone home. He was the only little guy left, and the nurses had been able to love on him lots while they waited for us to arrive.

Meeting each of our children for the first time was such an incredibly unique experience. Our first daughter was stillborn, so tiny at 20 weeks, with such extreme sadness and unspeakable loss surrounding her birth. Gabriel's delivery was difficult—he was a pretty big baby—resulting in a broken collar bone for him, a blood transfusion required for me, and the later discovery of his group B strep infection followed by a 16-day NICU stay. We had such fear and concern as sepsis settled in that this incredibly sick baby might not come home with us either. Kaleigh's delivery was rather unremarkable, except she was able to room-in with me for the entire stay, an experience I had not yet had. Her birth was quick and uncomplicated. Samuel's meet and greet was already elaborated on a bit, but the truth is, even though I hadn't given birth to him myself, and regardless of how many hours or days or weeks old he was, I knew with such a solid confidence he was meant to be ours.

Josiah's meeting was its own kind of unique and wonderful, more along the lines of the classic adoption moments seen in Instagram videos. We waited with anticipation in a room while the nurse brought the baby to us. She placed him in my arms and then left so we could have a few moments together. There really aren't words adequate enough to describe meeting your child for the first time, no matter how they come to you. Your heart swells with joy and hope, and it's both an emotional and physical reaction. What a gift!

We planned to stay at a hotel for a couple of days, but were given the option to room-in with Josiah at the hospital. Of course, we said yes! We were able to feed him and change his diapers and cuddle and coo and walk the halls those few days away from home.

Josiah's birth mother was still at the hospital when we arrived, and we caught a glimpse of her at the end of the hall at one point. She didn't want to meet us, and that was OK. We have always wanted to be respectful of the privacy of the expectant mothers and birth mothers we've interacted with, allowing them to determine the level of interaction and communication. It's not the easiest thing in the world for me to do. There's a bit of discomfort in not having any control over that aspect from our end, but we understood that this is how the adoption world currently works, and we were willing to follow someone else's lead, always. We were told by the nurses that she checked herself out of the hospital 24 hours after giving birth in order to go visit her eldest son (I believe he was 16 or 17 at the time.) who was ill in another hospital (It was indicated to us that he was hospitalized because of complications from Duchenne).

We did meet the boys' paternal grandmother while at the hospital. We found out she had not been able to meet Samuel while he was in temporary care waiting for a family. She showed up at the nurse's station and asked to see her grandson. It was a bit of an unusual situation, with birth mother not wanting contact, us not having met any family previously, and then she was just there, hoping to see him. The nurse escorted her into our room, mistakenly assuming she was related to us. Although confused and surprised for a moment, we didn't turn her away.

She seemed to be at peace with Josiah going home to join his brother and in knowing that the boys would be raised in a Christian household together. Despite the joy in holding her grandson, the interaction was brief. She didn't want to bother us, but she wanted to make sure to take this opportunity while it was even a possibility. There was so much sadness in her eyes and behind her smile.

We don't know much backstory about Samuel and Josiah's birth family; just where we arrive in the timeline. We were given a medical form filled out by their biological father with a tiny bit of family history: he's left handed, 5'9", no serious health concerns in the family, his mother is diabetic, he works as a carpenter, and that's really about it. We never got any medical or family history from the biological mother's side.

We also met the boys' birth father while at the hospital, which was definitely another surprise. His daughter, who was around 8 or 9 years old (and Samuel and Josiah's half sister), wanted to meet the baby. I think it was very admirable of him to want to do that for her, and very brave to be willing to meet us in order to make that happen. He asked at the nurse's station if a meeting could be arranged. Again, we didn't want to turn them away. Josiah wasn't legally ours yet anyway, and we certainly wanted to allow the opportunity for these family members to say both hello and goodbye. I can't imagine how that must feel.

We visited for a brief 20 to 30 minute period of time. Yes, it was awkward, but surprisingly, not unbearably so. He spoke a little bit about his other children (two older sons and this daughter), and told us about his work. We were careful not to share much personal information, speaking of our other children in generalities, and about our life and experience with vague descriptions of where, when, and how. He also had voiced no interest in ongoing communication, so we wanted to honor that for him, while offering our own selves a little layer of "protection" at the same time. It was nice, albeit incredibly bittersweet, to be able to offer his daughter a few moments with the little brother we assume she will never see again. Josiah's sister held him and talked to him, but I honestly don't remember if his father did. I don't remember him really asking much about Samuel either, other than in a very general way. I know he knew we had adopted Samuel, and I know he knew about his Duchenne diagnosis, but that wasn't discussed. A "nice to meet you," was said, and our time together was done.

Josiah passed every physical and medical check they needed in order to release him, so the hospital stay was over, and we headed home with a new baby in tow. Back home, we had to make some adjustments. Two of the upstairs bedrooms in our house were huge (14 x 18ish), and one was much smaller (8 x 10 or so). Gabriel and Kaleigh each had a large bedroom and when we moved Samuel from our bedroom into his own room at around a year old, he got the teeny tiny room. He was tiny too, so it seemed perfect. Once we found out we were going to have an additional little one in the house, Gabriel offered to give up his big room so the little boys could share it. Josiah slept in our bedroom for about a year as well. We did take Gabriel up on this sweet and thoughtful offer a bit later, and he moved into the much smaller space.

The big kids were thrilled to have another baby join the family. Samuel was still young enough that he didn't have much of a clue as to what was going on. He didn't have any idea how much his life was going to change as a "big brother." He was very excited and entertained to see this little guy wiggle and squeak. Josiah was an interesting creature to this curious toddler. Samuel's little buddy and permanent sidekick had arrived.

Becker Muscular Dystrophy, Congenital Muscular Dystrophy, Myotonic Muscular Dystrophy, and Limb-Girdle Muscular Dystrophy, among several others. There are a total of some 30 types which vary in severity and age of onset.

What is Duchenne?

Duchenne Muscular Dystrophy (often abbreviated DMD) is a fatal, progressive genetic disorder. It occurs because of a change in the dystrophin gene. There are 79 "exons" which serve as puzzle pieces in a chain. The changes to the gene can be deletions, mutations, or duplications. My boys both have a deletion of exons 5-7. These changes cause a disruption in the chain and then the genetic information can't be read properly by the body. The end result is a lack of dystrophin protein. These changes to the gene can happen at any point along that dystrophin chain.

Dystrophin protein acts likes the glue that holds muscles together. Typically when a person exercises, their muscles break down a little bit as a result of that work, and then build back up stronger. When dystrophin is missing, the muscle fibers break down and can't repair themselves. The healthy muscle is replaced by fatty fibrous tissue. Progressive weakness and degeneration of the skeletal muscles follow. The lack of dystrophin affects all muscles of the body (skeletal, cardiac, pulmonary).

When was Duchenne first discovered?

Duchenne was first described by two Italian doctors (Giovanni Semmola in 1834 and Gaetano Conte in 1836). However,

Duchenne is named after the French neurologist, Guillaume-Benjamin-Amand Duchenne, who described it fully in a book in 1861. He studied boys with Duchenne for years. He was also the first to do a biopsy of tissue of a Duchenne patient to examine under a microscope. It wasn't until much, much later (1980s) that further real scientific discovery came about, leading to additions and improvements to the standard of care.

How common is Duchenne?

Duchenne is considered a rare disease, occurring in approximately 1 in 5,000 male births. Duchenne is the most common form of muscular dystrophy. It is also considered to be the most common fatal genetic disorder among children.

Male births - it's just boys?

Here's a bit of a genetics lesson—because the dystrophin gene is found on the x-chromosome, it affects males because they only have one x-chromosome (male= x and y, female= x and x), and therefore Duchenne is inherited from the mother. Females can be carriers. Some carriers may end up with a varying range of Duchenne's physical symptoms, and they are called "manifesting" carriers. However, the mother does not always end up being diagnosed as a carrier, as spontaneous mutations of the dystrophin gene occur in approximately 30% of cases.

When does diagnosis happen?

Most of what I've read indicates diagnosis typically occurs

between 3 and 5 years old, based on developmental milestones not being met, weakness, falling, toe walking, or Gower's maneuver [rising to a standing position while "walking" hands up legs for support]. Other signs can be a waddling gait, enlarged calves, and lumbar lordosis (inward curve of the spine). Apparently some boys are not diagnosed until 7 or 8 years old. I have heard of some taking a very long time to finally reach an accurate diagnosis. Samuel was diagnosed just after birth using a blood sample and genetic sequencing. Testing was indicated because of family history: His birth mother had an uncle with Duchenne, a brother with Duchenne, and another son (half brother to Samuel and Josiah) with Duchenne. Then, of course, we had Josiah tested as an infant as well.

How do you confirm a diagnosis?

Coupled with suspicions from a pediatrician, parent, or teacher, a high creatine kinase (CK) level can be an indicator of Duchenne (or other muscle damage) and is often the first step in testing, but it does not give a definitive diagnosis. A muscle biopsy can also be done—studying the muscle fibers under a microscope to determine dystrophin expression—although it's my understanding it is not necessarily common at this point to have a muscle biopsy done (our boys have not). Genetic testing is strongly encouraged, not only to get a definitive diagnosis, but also to determine what specific type of mutation is present. This is important information to have as many mutation-specific therapies are in development.

What is the lifespan of someone with Duchenne?

Currently, the average lifespan of someone living with Duchenne is around 27 years old. This has improved over the last decade or so as more consistent medical care has been made available along with advances in heart and lung support. Many die younger, and some live longer, but early- to mid-twenties is usually considered typical.

What treatments are available?

There is no cure for Duchenne and few treatments exist. There are so many amazing drugs and therapies in the pipeline, and there is much hope for the future. This can't happen soon enough, but clinical trials and the drug development process are slow, complicated, and so incredibly expensive.

A multi-layered or "cocktail" approach to treatment appears to be favored by many at this point. However, none of those are, or look at this point like they will be, an actual cure. Corticosteroids are the current standard of care—Various types and protocols exist (daily, high dose weekend, 10 days on/10 days off)—and several studies show that the boys and young men who are on steroids typically fare better for longer (maintaining ambulation, lung function, etc.). When taking steroids long term there is always the possibility for side effects which needs to be taken into consideration: weight gain, shorter stature, increased risk of bone fractures, cataracts, insulin resistance, and 'roid rage—anger induced by steroid use. Because of these, some families choose to never use steroids at all. Exon skipping drugs, gene therapy, steroid alternatives, stem cell replacement, and others are all on the table and in various phases of development.

Supplements are encouraged. Although there are a variety of opinions on how many, which ones, and what doses, I can tell you our boys currently take daily multivitamins, probiotics, CoQ10, vitamin D (boys with Duchenne typically have low vitamin D levels), their weekend dosing of steroids, and the recent addition of an ACE inhibitor. We try to feed them a diet healthy in fruits and vegetables, whole grains, and low in sugar, but the truth is they sometimes get ice cream and chicken nuggets, good ol' boxed mac 'n' cheese, all the "kid stuff." We definitely just try to outweigh those more questionable choices with super healthy ones.

Physical therapy, aqua therapy, and even equine therapy can be beneficial. None of the therapies should focus on strength building, because that can end up being more damaging to muscles. However, gentle stretching and massage, range of motion, and balancing activities can prove to be extremely helpful.

Night-time AFOs (ankle-foot orthoses) are recommended—aka night splints. I have also heard them called night boots or moon boots. These help keep the foot and ankle flexed to a 90-degree angle which gives a good stretch overnight or whenever they are worn. This is beneficial because the heel cords tend to get very tight and eventually cause toe walking and different posturing to compensate, leading to balance issues and an increased fall risk. As progression continues, hand splints are often used as well.

Why is there no cure?

Any disease takes money, time, and a lot of research to come up with treatments and a potential cure—How long have they been working on a cure for cancer?—With the designation of Duchenne as a rare disease, it's even harder to get the funding to proceed with drug formulation and clinical trials and to convince pharmaceutical companies this is worth their effort and expense with such a small population to treat.

The exon skipping therapies are available for those with a deletion amenable to skipping the most common exons (as of this writing, exons 51, 53 and 45). The most frequently occurring is exon 51, with approximately 13% of Duchenne boys potentially benefitting from that particular exon skipping drug. Samuel and Josiah could potentially benefit from skipping exon 8. Skipping 8 would allow the dystrophin "puzzle pieces" to fit together again, just missing a section—in their case 5-7, forcing a skip of 8. For them, this would allow exons 4 and 9 to match up as the "puzzle pieces" in the dystrophin protein to complete the chain, in theory producing some dystrophin to be read and used by the body, albeit a shorter chain. Approximately 2% of Duchenne boys would benefit from skipping exon 8, so it's further down on the priority list for drug manufacturers—number eight in order of "importance," I believe.

As mentioned previously, clinical trials are ongoing for so many areas: steroid alternatives, medications that boost the mitochondria as the powerhouse of the cell, anti-inflammatory options, gene therapy, etc. An additional piece to this is that the flawed gene that causes Duchenne wasn't identified until 1986. The dystrophin protein was identified and named in 1987. So although that's already been 35 years, in the grand scheme of things, Duchenne research is still in relatively early stages.

What is the progression of Duchenne?

This varies, even among those with the same deletion or in the same family. Weakness is seen typically by 3 to 5 years old through the pelvis (which leads to the aforementioned waddling gait). Some boys never run. Progressive weakness leads to loss of ambulation and full-time wheelchair use on average by 10 to 13 years old. Some amount of support is usually needed prior to that, such as a medical stroller, scooter, or manual wheelchair, especially for longer distances or tiring days like zoo trips, amusement parks, museums, or for use during a typical school day.

Stairs become difficult and eventually impossible, and weakness can lead to more frequent falls and an increased concern for fracture. Many boys who are losing strength and experience a fall resulting in a fracture in the leg or ankle end up never walking again. A weakening of the torso and shoulders follows, and feeding themselves becomes difficult. Once in a wheelchair full-time, additional concerns for positioning arise, both for comfort and care, and scoliosis is common.

Through the teen years, heart and lung involvement and further weakening of the muscles of the arms and torso complicate daily activities and self-care. As Duchenne progresses, heart and lung weakness worsen, making pneumonia and even the common cold dangerous. Enter in cough assist machines, bipap, other assisted ventilation, Hoyer lifts, shower chairs, hospital beds, and rotating mattresses to avoid bedsores. All of the things.

What behavioral and learning concerns might there be in conjunction with a Duchenne diagnosis?

While certainly not all are affected, there is generally a higher incidence of learning disabilities, anger/argumentative behavior, depression, memory concerns, speech delay, ADHD, autism, anxiety, OCD, and sensory issues. Despite loads of research, there still is not much (or enough) known about the effect the lack of dystrophin has on a developing brain.

My two boys are excellent students, extremely verbal, and we currently have zero academic concerns. They have amazing fine motor skills and are much more gifted artistically than anyone else in our household. They are walking encyclopedias of animal facts, and their vocabulary and reasoning skills impress me daily.

However, they both have had periods of aggressive outbursts and anger. They don't do well with transitions, so we accommodate by laying out the plan for the day, always with the accompanying announcement that things MAY change, a five minute heads up for moving on to something new, and verbal reminders about going to the bathroom/getting shoes on, even though that definitely is the routine every time we leave the house to go anywhere.

We have learned what is likely to trigger an outburst or belligerence and plan ahead as best we can to avoid or be able to tone it down, at least much of the time. When they're tired, we offer a bit of grace, but at the same time, it's never appropriate to be inappropriate. It's always so hard to tell if these episodes are related to fatigue or discomfort in their bodies, the fact that we're dealing with 6- and 8-year old boys, their own inborn personalities, or the weekly steroids wreaking havoc on their systems. We do the best we can and keep learning as we go along.

Both Samuel and Josiah have some OCD tendencies, espe-cially Josiah at this point. These are nothing crippling to his day, but some examples are: straightening the pillows on the couch if they're not "just so," making sure the seams on his socks match up in a straight line before putting on his shoes, or scooting his chair forward at the table to just the right spot. We try to be patient with these things, realizing that he really can't help it, and yet, sometimes it adds a little time to moving on with the day. We do our best to just go with it when we can. He has only recently been able to verbalize that "it didn't look (or feel) right and I didn't like it, so I had to fix it."

They both also have some sensory issues, especially Samuel. Neither of them wear clothing with buttons, snaps, or zippers. We buy nothing with a collar and only the softest of T-shirt material or the slickest of athletic wear will do. Drawstrings on the inside of pants are troublesome for Josiah, meanwhile Samuel doesn't wear underwear anymore. We tried boxers, briefs, boxer briefs, a size too large, and different types of material, all to no avail. It's OK, commando it is.

Neither of them are comfortable in tennis shoes. We have tried loose and sloppy vs. properly fitted with good support. Instead, they wear Crocs year round—no socks for Samuel, socks with perfectly even lines for Josiah!.

Pants are difficult to find for Samuel. His sensory concerns coupled with the large size of his calves mean that at the end of each summer I order something like 20 pairs of athletic style pants from various stores to allow him to try them on, make his assessment, and deem one or two "acceptable." I then buy multiple colors of those in his current size and return all of the rest. It would be easier if the fit was the same from year to year, but changes in his leg size and shape means we basically end up starting from scratch each year for pants.

The boys both tend to be hot bodies. If we would let them, they'd probably wear shorts all year long. We drag it out as long as possible into the fall, pairing shorts and a T-shirt with a jacket so I don't get too many dirty looks about letting my children out of the house half-dressed. Then the season arrives when we come to an agreement: "If we're going out, you must wear long pants." When we return home, getting back into shorts or pajamas is fine.

Pajamas for them tend to be extremely oversized T-shirts and athletic shorts (back to those drawstring rules, however!). As soon as we return home from PT, the grocery store, or wherever we might have been, they ask if we are home for the day. If the answer is yes, they'll happily put their pajamas on as early as they can. I can't blame them for loving comfort!

None of these sensory needs are life altering. It can be troublesome when the boys have outgrown something and we can't find the proper replacement because the brand has changed the style or fit or discontinued that particular item entirely. We've learned what they tolerate and what is upsetting and difficult for them and we make the adjustments as we can to keep them comfortable. We definitely know where it is I need to typically shop for their clothes.

Both Samuel and Josiah have had periods of difficulty with emotions. Josiah tends to be a bit more moody on a day-to-day basis. I believe this is in part from wanting things to go his way and being extremely disappointed when they don't, and in part not understanding how the world or this particular household works. Then he becomes angry or belligerent as he navigates through that learning curve—maybe typical kid stuff?

Samuel is much more generally easy going and content in attitude and behavior. However, about every four to six months he has an outburst of emotion he can't explain. He'll cry and scream and be both angry and sad at the same time. Sometimes we can figure out what trigger took him over the edge, and other times it's purely a mystery. He sobs and wraps himself in his blanket and wants to lay on his bed and asks to be alone for a bit. It's hard for me to see him so sad and miserable. When he's had some time to work through it and get back to mellow, he's wiped out for the day. He'll sometimes say he was just sad and he doesn't know why, but he needed to cry. I guess I get it, sometimes I just need to cry too.

What other medical issues should I be aware of?

Of course, this can vary, depending on what other medical diagnoses might be involved. The neuromuscular team should always be consulted with questions. These are just bits I've learned over time and have made mental note of in regard to specific concerns in Duchenne.

In general, with Duchenne, there needs to be an awareness of rhabdomyolysis (rapid breakdown of muscle) which can be caused by overexertion and dehydration or after inhaled anesthesia is used. This can cause permanent kidney damage and be life threatening. Milder instances can be resolved with aggressive hydration. One of the primary symptoms of rhabdomyolysis is dark or cola colored urine. However, rhabdomyolysis is always something to be taken very seriously. If hydration does not return the urine to normal color quickly, it's imperative to get checked out at the ER. Our boys have each experienced this a couple of times; too much activity at an indoor water park, running and playing at a friend's small farm. Each time it resolved quickly, but it was concerning nonetheless.

Inhaled anesthesia can cause rhabdomyolysis. Succhiny-choline should never be given to someone with Duchenne, but other inhaled anesthetics have also proven to be problematic. Intravenous anesthesia should be used whenever possible.

Fat embolism syndrome is also a concern. This can occur when a bone is broken (more likely with "long bones" like the femur). It is believed that when the bone is broken, small pieces of fat break free and enter the bloodstream. This is especially dangerous if the fat emboli travel to the lungs.

Those who are on daily steroid dosing are considered to be immune compromised. In emergency situations (if they miss their typical dosing by more than 24 hours, they have had vomiting and not been able to keep down their medications, or just due to the extra stress the body is under due to various circumstances), they may need to have a stress dose of steroids given at the hospital. Live vaccines should also not be given to those on daily dosing. Steroids should also never be stopped suddenly. Instead, tapering down the dosage is necessary to prevent adrenal concerns.

Cough/cold medicines need to be carefully considered. Pseu-doephedrine should not be given (active ingredient in Sudafed), while Mucinex is recommended.

Both of my boys have medical ID bracelets which list their name, date of birth, their Duchenne diagnosis, no succhiny-choline, no inhaled anesthesia, high dose weekend steroids, and my phone number for an emergency contact. After a lot of reading and research, I hope we hit the highlights of what should be included for emergency purposes.

What does a care team look like?

We have a family doctor (a nurse practitioner, to be precise). The family practice provides for the boys' well visits, immunizations, and common everyday ailments. Truthfully, they have a very limited knowledge of Duchenne, and I wouldn't have expected them to, especially before meeting our boys. However, we have also done a lot of educating along the way at that office.

I think this just comes along with the responsibility of advocating for your child. You educate as best you can in order for your child's care to be the best it can be. It is a rare disease after all. Physicians who don't specialize in Duchenne care generally aren't super well-informed about the particular needs and concerns. You hope to be able to have an honest and respectful dialogue with the professional who actually knows quite a bit less than you in this particular regard. You live the reality of Duchenne every day. However, it's also always a partnership in working toward the best care possible. We are incredibly fortunate that our boys are generally very healthy, so we don't have much need outside of those well visits for the general practitioner's office at this point.

We also have a physical therapist the boys have been seeing for about six years. Physical therapists with specific experience with or who are really well-versed in care specific to Duchenne are few and far between. We didn't know of, nor could we find, any near where we live. We took a chance on a part-time pediatric physical therapist who works from her home who we met through the kids' dance studio (Point of interest, this studio is owned by Ruth, the mother to Leah who called us about Samuel in the first place.).

It has turned out to be an ideal situation. The fact that it's a non-clinical setting gets bonus points from me. Scheduling is rather easy, and we just work it out. When either family is on vacation, it's no big deal to cancel. When Miss Christina had to have physical therapy of her own for a shoulder injury, we reworked our schedule. If one of us is sick, we cancel easily. I believe she had previously worked for a time with someone with Duchenne, but regardless, she certainly has been open to listening to what we've learned and putting into practice particular suggestions we've made. She has also done a lot of research on her own, had conversations with other physical therapists, and participated in webinars specific to Duchenne. We appreciate the efforts she's made to serve our family, and she is really very good at her job.

Then there's the team we see at Lurie Children's Hospital: pediatric neurologist, cardiologist, pulmonologist, dietetics/bone health, a clinic nurse, orthotics, PT, OT (I think that's all of them?). I'll explain more about that in Chapter 5 in describing a clinic visit.

As Duchenne progresses, many families arrange for personal care assistants, additional nursing care in the home, or make use of respite. Some families take on the care of their sons all on their own, with additional education and training along the way as equipment is added. At this point, we are still a distance away from that chapter of our lives, so this is an area I know very little about.

Where can I go to learn more about Duchenne?

We learned very early on that a general internet search can lead to outdated and frightening information (from back in the days when parents were told, "There's nothing you can do. Take them home and love them."). We were quickly able to weed out the nonsense and get to the websites and organizations which are up-to-date with research and advocacy and education. I would recommend four in particular:

Parent Project Muscular Dystrophy (PPMD) www.Parent-Projectmd.org.

This is one of the first websites we found with solid information. It is Duchenne parent founded, as well as Duchenne parent supported. PPMD is heavily involved in advocacy, education, and fundraising to support research. We were able to attend the annual national conference just weeks after adopting Samuel, benefiting from a scholarship for newly diagnosed families. Samuel was unique in that he was diagnosed so very young, by far the youngest with Duchenne present at the conference. This made him a bit of a "star," if you will. We met some other families, sat in on educational workshops about setting up a care team, and heard about research and development ongoing for potential treatments. We lived and breathed this new Duchenne world for four days, for good or for bad; mostly good.

In addition to an annual conference, PPMD also hosts smaller regional workshops throughout the year. Cory and I have been fortunate to be able to attend several. Additionally, we have participated in some fundraising for PPMD, partnering as charity runners for the Shamrock Shuffle 8k, Rock 'n' Roll 5k and Half Marathon, and the Chicago Marathon. PPMD also partners with neuromuscular clinics to set an exceptional standard of care across the board. "Certified Duchenne Care Centers" are given this label after meeting that standard. Families who receive care at these facilities can be assured they will be able to expect the same level of care as at any other of these certified centers.

Cure Duchenne www.cureduchenne.org.

This website is also full of accurate, up-to-date information. Cure Duchenne is also Duchenne parent founded and Duchenne parent supported. There is a large focus on funding research and seeking adequate and effective treatments (along with partnerships with pharmaceutical companies, similar to these other organizations), but there is also a strong education and advocacy focus. Cure Duchenne appears to be intent on getting in on ground-level funding for promising treatments. We have attended a couple of Cure Duchenne's regional workshops and one national conference.

Jett Foundation www.jettfoundation.org.

My perception is that the Jett Foundation is more focused on education and assistance, with a push for research always present, but more in the background. It is also Duchenne parent founded and Duchenne parent supported. The Jett Foundation hosts educational workshops, some support group activities (Porch Nite), and a summer camp specifically for Duchenne boys and young men called Camp Promise. There is also a charitable arm of the organization with assistance funds (emergency basis—meeting rent/utility/food needs, and a separate accessible vehicle fund with an application process available each year to a limited number of families).

Muscular Dystrophy Association (MDA) www.mda.org.

The MDA has been around for such a long time and has some great programs for education and support. Of course, the MDA is a heavy hitter in the world of research, in part because of the name recognition and longevity. The MDA represents all neuromuscular diseases (ALS, Spinal Muscular Atrophy, and many, many others, in addition to Duchenne). The previous organizations I listed above focus solely on Duchenne and/or its close brother Becker Muscular Dystrophy. One of the biggest direct benefits we've experienced with the MDA is through the neuromuscular clinic. Our boys see the team at the MDA clinic at Lurie Children's Hospital in Chicago (which is also a Certified Duchenne Care Center through PPMD).

There are many other websites with current information, and I know of a few others that offer financial assistance specific to Duchenne families for home modifications or to help with the cost of medical equipment that insurance may not fully cover. These four are the biggies for me.

Five

Clinic Visits and Research

We go to MDA Clinic Day at Lurie Children's Hospital in Chicago twice a year. In the weeks prior to each visit we stop by a local lab for blood draws and urine samples. These test for glucose levels, calcium, vitamin D, among other things. The results are sent on to the hospital for review.

On clinic day, Samuel and Josiah are scheduled at the same appointment time and both Cory and I make the journey to Chicago with them. We don't visit Chicago too often, but when we do, it's usually driving up there at a low-traffic time. The appointment for clinic is always at 8:30 am on a Thursday (definitely NOT a low-traffic time!). With no traffic, we live about an hour away from the hospital. With morning rush hour, we always plan for one and a half to two hours, so it's a good thing the boys are early risers! On those days, we get up, get dressed, and head out with breakfast in hand.

The drive is usually nothing dramatic, with Cory always at the helm. We park in the garage, stop at the reception desk to receive our visitor passes for the day, then ride the elevator up to the pediatric neurology unit. We check in there and have height, weight, and blood pressure taken. Then they show us to our rooms. We always request that the two of us each have our own exam room with one of the boys by our side (so far, I have had Samuel with me at each visit, and Cory has had Josiah as his buddy for the day).

We tried all four of us in the same exam room at one point and it was a disaster (at least from my perspective)! We had two very active little boys, two parents, and multiple providers in and out of the room asking questions about both boys at the same time. To me it felt like a lot of chaos. "Divide and conquer" makes all of us calmer and more cooperative, while in theory, not taking up any more of the staff's time than we would have all together anyway.

It's a pretty streamlined way of being able to meet with multiple specialties in a relatively short time. We sit in our assigned room and the staff members come to us. The cardiologist may be in speaking with me and Samuel while the neurologist is in the room with Cory and Josiah. All the records are computerized, of course, so they can also reference each other's notes as they go.

We typically see a neurologist, cardiologist, pulmonologist, dietitian/bone health specialist, occupational therapist, physical therapist, orthotist, nurse, and an MDA staff person. Depending on the schedule and the boys' particular needs at the time, we head to various departments for testing (EKG, echocardiogram, DEXA scan–which looks at bone density, and various pulmonary function tests). Additional tests will be added on as the boys age and their condition progresses: cardiac MRI and sleep study, among others.

Over a period of approximately four to five hours these specialists rotate between our two rooms and gather as much information as they can. In that relatively short period of time, they ask about how the boys have been doing for the previous six months. They ask about changes in our home, what school progress looks like, how often we see the physical therapist, and what kinds of things they do during their sessions with her. They ask about how often the boys wear their night splints and check for whether or not they still fit well or if we need a new prescription. They compare notes with the updated assessment from our physical therapist. The boys are timed on how long it takes them to get up from the floor, how quickly they can walk down the hall, and how well they can balance on one foot.

The staff share the results of the boys' blood work with us and discuss any changes needed in the amount of Vitamin D supplementation we give them, or if the steroid dosage needs to be adjusted due to size and weight increase over time. We discuss the boys' diets and how many servings of dairy, red meat, fruits, and vegetables they consume in an average week. They listen to their heart and lungs, and posture is checked for the potential beginning of scoliosis. We discuss the results of the bone density scan, cardiology report (Is there any scarring yet on Samuel's heart?), and any changes in their overall health, stamina, or gait that we may have noticed since the last appointment.

These appointments are in no way interesting to the boys, and it can be agony to basically be in the same room either on an exam table or in a very standard issue plastic medical office chair for hours on end. How do we remedy that? Samuel and Josiah each have a "bag of tricks" prepared for the day. In the week or so before the appointments we stop by Target and pick some activity books or toys from the dollar bin section, a new LEGO set each, and some special snacks—treats we don't normally purchase, such as fruit snacks, chocolate covered granola bars—along with a notebook and some colored pens. They're all set for the day. Samuel and Josiah each have a large tote bag with all these goodies, plus their night braces. Some of the staff have told us we are one of the most prepared families that comes to clinic. I tell them I simply see it as a survival tactic!

Cory and I touch base a day or two before we go in order to recap our thoughts on the boys' current status: Have there been more "'roid rage" moments lately? Has Samuel been tired and asked for more frequent rides in his medical stroller? Have either of them complained of leg pain? How do they each compare to their peers at this point? What changes have there been from what we remember them each doing six months prior?

We review their weekend steroid dosage and make a list of the supplements they currently take so there's no thinking required in the moment with the doctors. Do we have any questions? Are there changes we've noticed or anticipate happening soon that need to be addressed with the addition of any equipment?

We feel as prepared as we possibly can be. We certainly could reach out in between appointments with questions or concerns, but Cory and I agree the more we can cover during the appointment time, the less likely we would need additional assistance in between. Cory is an amazingly fun dad and an aware father. Although he often works long hours and the bulk of the day-to-day parenting falls to me, he's fully aware of the boys' current abilities and challenges. Cory is completely on top of things. He's a participant in their care, a partner in parenting, and he can confidently comment on Josiah's status with the professionals.

As of right now (winter 2022), our boys are doing exceedingly well. We feel it, but it's also been confirmed by the clinicians. We have some pretty amazing insurance provided to us by the church, and the boys are both currently participating in physical therapy sessions three times a week. That alone is a huge blessing.

During the dreaded COVID-time (I hate that I'm even commenting on COVID, but it's important to note), other patients seen through Lurie's clinic received zero services for months on end (PT, OT, speech, and others), or were only able to receive services via telehealth sessions. Meanwhile, during the peak of COVID was when our insurance approved moving from twice weekly sessions to three PT sessions each week. This may be a bit controversial due to COVID mandates and protocols that have been in place at various times, but frankly, it's a simple fact: We never stopped receiving in-person services. There have been other times (an illness in our family or when our physical therapist was sick) when we did need to participate via telehealth. My personal opinion is that it's likely better than nothing, but there is truly no comparison to the benefit provided by in-person care, especially with the hands-on aspect of physical therapy. It certainly also reduces this mama's frustration when having to play tutor/coach/middle man during that type of session.

Can I even say this?…We were told at our visit in November 2021 (20 months after the beginning of COVID lockdowns and restrictions) that our two sons are the only patients they see at that particular clinic who did not have losses—at that time they were stable. So many of the boys/young men had SIGNIFICANT loss of skill/ambulation/strength. And in the world of Duchenne, stable is as good as you can ask for. Stable requires celebration. That simple statement moved me beyond words. We do the best we can each day. We take advice from the professionals. We read, research, and ask questions. We pray. We slog through parenting, homeschooling, and medical concerns and hope that we are making the right decisions in all those areas as we go, questioning ourselves every step of the way.

We were so very pleased to hear that from them. At the same time, we were so immensely saddened to know how many Duchenne boys (let alone all the other multitudes of people who receive a variety of services elsewhere) were failed during lockdowns, protocols, and mitigations. I can't imagine the frustration and helplessness felt by the parents of those kids and the professionals who serve them. Their hands were tied. Especially in boys and young men with Duchenne, these are skills they will not get back. There are not gains to be made, only further loss. That news devastated me.

As part of the experience at Lurie, the medical team usually has some sort of conversation with us about what current or upcoming trials their clinic is participating in and whether or not Samuel and Josiah would likely be eligible. From the very beginning we have been interested in participating in anything we can, or at least hoping to have an in-depth conversation about what those options entail. This is not only to potentially benefit our sons (although the direct benefit is often not received by those participating in studies or clinical trials), but to ultimately help forward the research. The Duchenne population is small enough, that in order to attempt to move drug trials forward and to complete studies on any number of things, a large number of families need to be willing to participate.

Samuel was recruited to be part of a trial when he was very young. This particular trial was looking at early steroid use in a Duchenne population under 2 years old. We discussed it at his first clinic visit when he was around 6 months old. We were very interested, but found out the hospital's ethics board would not allow his participation until his adoption was finalized. He ended up enrolling in the study right at 1 year old.

The protocol was using high dose weekends—receiving the same amount of corticosteroid that normally would be prescribed over a seven day period, except split over two days. It's my understanding that it was becoming one of the standard protocols at that time. Steroid dosing still doesn't typically begin until around 4 years old or later. Many boys aren't diagnosed until around that age and/or some physicians recommend waiting until physical skill has "plateaued" before beginning a corticosteroid regimen.

Samuel tolerated the protocol well. We simply put his dose in with the formula in his bottle on weekends with no issue. Once Josiah came around, we were offered opportunity to use the same protocol for him. The trial was completed by that time, but we opted to go ahead and start him on a corticosteroid regimen at 6 months old. Now they drink their weekend "medicine" right out of the little dosing cups along with their breakfast and the other supplements they take.

The boys have not been a part of any other formal clinical trial to this point, although there had been discussion about them being prime candidates for gene therapy, and they were both pre-screened for one trial in particular. Due to FDA and COVID delays, Samuel aged out of that opportunity. We recently found out that neither of the boys are eligible at this point for any of the current gene therapy trials due to their deletion (exons 5-7). Some adverse events were recorded from other boys with "earlier in the dystrophin chain" exon deletions, so they have limited who can be screened with this as one of the current criteria. There may be a stem cell treatment trial in the future as a possibility, but it's too soon to know at this point.

Cory and I have participated in numerous surveys for Duchenne families, ranging from caregiver burden, to "how did you tell your other children about your son's diagnosis," to inquiring about our base knowledge of each of the approved treatments and their efficacy. I took part in a roundtable discussion about various corticosteroids and their perceived advantages and benefits over one another. Gabriel and Kaleigh have also participated in some sibling surveys.

Samuel was part of an MRI study looking at the function of the calf muscle. He was also part of a study investigating sleep quality and duration in boys with Duchenne which implemented a family education program to set him up for success. We look for as many of these opportunities as we can, because we feel the burden and responsibility to participate fully in the process in order to help our boys, or to at least further the cause for the boys who will follow.

There is still so much not known about Duchenne. As a parent, it's reassuring to know there are so many researchers, biotech/pharmaceutical companies, and physicians working toward bettering life for all the boys and young men with Duchenne. Treatments can't come soon enough.

Six

A Lesson in Love

After we shared news of the boys' diagnosis with our congregation, we received such immense support. Generosity was offered not only through the giving of financial donations to PPMD's cause as part of the Shamrock Shuffle, but kindnesses were shown in many other ways: the promise of prayer, offers if we "ever needed anything for the boys" to please come to them, and questions asked wanting to genuinely know more about Duchenne.

A month or two after that big reveal, the Elders of the congregation approached Cory at the end of a meeting. "Pastor, we want to talk to you about something." Uh-oh, the thoughts that flashed through his mind with that open-ended introduction! "We're wondering what needs to happen with the house for the boys."

We live in a parsonage. If you don't know, a parsonage is a

house provided to the pastor's family by the congregation. The congregation owns it and is responsible for its upkeep, and the pastor and his family live in that house for the duration of their time serving at that congregation.

Our parsonage at the time of this conversation was approximately 140 years old and had served the previous 14 pastors well. It had been updated and added on to a couple of times through those years and in general, had been pretty well-maintained over that time. With four bedrooms, two bathrooms, and a rather large yard, it had been a nice home for us for several years already.

The concern the Elders had was space for eventual accessibility needs: an appropriate and useful bathroom, enough room for the turning radius required by power wheelchairs, and the ability for the boys to be a part of the family by using the entirety of the house while not being cordoned off to their own "wing" if an accessible addition were to be built. Although our home had served our previous family of four rather well, and so many pastors' families before that, adding two more children and surveying the layout of the home now posed some concerns for the boys' future needs. The house had small-ish compartmentalized rooms, three of the four bedrooms were up a set of steep and very narrow stairs, and doorways throughout were not wide enough for a wheelchair to navigate.

When we first met with the social worker about Samuel's potential adoption, we knew this would become an eventual concern. There was brief discussion with her at that time about the possibility of building an addition to the north of the house. We didn't know then how much longer we would necessarily be living in this same place. (In our particular denomination, pastors can receive and accept a "call" to another congregation at any time. They have the option to accept or decline. It's common to have several different calls throughout your career, but some pastors stay put for years and years.) We planned to address it when it became necessary. However, we are very appreciative that the congregation brought the question to us when they did out of love and concern.

The discussion moved on to what to do and when. Knowing it would likely still be several years until an accommodating space needed to be available, they wanted to get the ball rolling on conversation with the congregation as a whole. In a church setting such as this, smaller decisions are made by individual committees or boards. With something as big as the consideration of changes to the parsonage, all of the congregation members needed the opportunity to have a voice.

At the next quarterly Voter's meeting, the Elders brought the question forward to the attendees. After brief discussion, an exploration committee was formed to research, lay out options, and come back with suggestions. Over a period of several months, those committee members completed an in-depth tour of the parsonage, making note of electrical and foundation concerns and the general condition of the house, in addition to surveying the space available and raising concerns about where the bedrooms and bathrooms were located. They then met with a couple of different architects and discussed the options to add-on, remodel, or demolish and rebuild.

In the end, it was recommended that due to the age of the building, those particular concerns noted above, and in part, a caution that "you never know what you'll find when you start opening up walls," the better demonstration of good stewardship would be to start from scratch. The congregation again held a meeting to specifically discuss the committee's findings. A vote was taken, and the decision was made to follow the committee's recommendations: A new build would happen.

At that point, another committee (with a few overlapping members from the previous group) was appointed to explore a floor plan, weigh the options between modular housing vs. traditional construction, and come up with an overall estimate with cost comparisons. Over the next few months, meetings continued. They were time consuming, but extremely productive. Cory and I were blessed to be invited to be a part of both the exploration and building committees. They were very open to our ideas and input. They trusted our research in regard to the medical and physical needs the boys will eventually have. I spent a lot of time talking with others who have remodeled or built accessible homes, specifically those with children with Duchenne: What is the ideal shower size? What would you have done differently? What are the minimum recommended dimensions for bedrooms? What are the important considerations for down the line when they are fully wheelchair dependent?

Although vitally important and so very informative, this part of the process was a bit difficult at times. I had excitement about these new plans and an appreciation for the congregation's forward thinking. At the same time, in asking these questions and looking to future needs, Duchenne was placed in the forefront of my thoughts on a daily basis. I had moments when telling the basics of our story yet again to a complete stranger to confirm what I'd learned about the building process and accessibility options gave me pause:

"Is this really happening?"

"I wish we didn't need to even be having this conversation."

"I so appreciate the wealth of information I've been able to find, but I don't have time to think about what the future holds for my little guys."

"It's so far away. I don't need to worry now. I should just be thankful for the opportunity to put things in place to make their lives as comfortable and easy as possible." (Comfortable and easy being a matter of perspective, of course.)

All of these thoughts appeared and reappeared throughout the process, intermingled with a gratitude and peace that plans were moving forward. We would have a safe place for them to live, knowing the people here love our family and care so deeply about our boys.

Some of the things that we had to consider were:

-How wide should the space around the kitchen island be for Samuel to navigate the perimeter in a wheelchair?

-What dimensions should the shower have to allow room for a reclining shower chair and a companion for when Josiah can no longer bathe himself?

-Do we want the master bedroom near the boys' rooms so that we can hear them call out in the night to help them turn in bed when they can no longer do it themselves? Or do we want to allow our bedroom to serve as a little oasis away from the daily needs on the other side of the house (using an intercom/google home type device for the boys to communicate their needs to us when we might not hear)?

-What size table do we want to have for our family of six, allowing more eventual space needed for two power chairs and adding in a few guests as we wish? What kind of table legs and what height for the top?

-At what height should light switches be placed?

-What type of flooring will be most durable long term for a busy, active family and two power chairs? There's a lot of variance, but each wheelchair can easily weigh 200+lb plus the weight of the occupant, so that's potentially a LOT of wear and tear on a floor.

And on, and on, and on…so many questions to answer, so many decisions to make. A crystal ball would have been helpful. Instead, I made use of Google searches and Facebook groups.

I've always been really good at making decisions, having an opinion, and pretty much sticking with it. I so often have a hard time describing what it is that I like, but I know it when I see it. Cory and I prepared for the discussions at each meeting, relayed new information, listened to conversation, and waited for the committee to come to their conclusions based on what information had been gathered. Typically, they would discuss a topic as a group, and Cory and I would sit back a bit. Once they narrowed it down to their top couple of choices (even for simple things like kitchen cabinet hardware), they'd ask our opinions, and we would weigh in with our thoughts and preferences. Overall, it was a smooth process from start to finish. The committee worked as a mostly cohesive group, and conversation was pleasant and civil throughout.

The committee relied heavily on our information and research, especially when looking at the functionality of the home as a whole. We read and researched. We sought answers from multiple resources. We read some more and asked follow-up questions. At one point, a committee member said, "Wow, you guys really have done your homework. I never would have thought to ask some of these questions!" My response was simply that we understood this was a serious task and an immense commitment for the congregation's finances. That definitely put a responsibility on us to be thorough, because no one wants to have to revisit the project in five or ten years and say, "Oops, we should have done it differently." The most minute details were important!

A plan was drafted, revised, brought to the congregation, and eventually approved. Fundraising efforts were ongoing: a pork fest and a dinner auction, among other things. We moved to a rental house exactly one mile from our home and settled in for however long the building process might take.

Up to this point, we had noted that Samuel moved a little slower than his peers. His running gait appeared a bit labored. He tired more quickly on a playground or when playing in our yard, but had always done a really good job of self-regulating and taking breaks as needed. The rental house had a master bedroom downstairs and two bedrooms upstairs. We quickly made the decision that the stairs were becoming difficult enough for him to navigate that climbing up and down multiple times a day wasn't any longer a good plan. He slept downstairs in the master bedroom with me for the time we lived there, while the big kids shared a bedroom, and Josiah and Cory shared the other bedroom. Although maybe not ideal, we certainly made it work for the time we needed.

In the middle of this planning process, we also began working with Make-A-Wish. Due to their Duchenne diagnosis, both boys are eligible to have a wish granted. Each state has its own Make-A-Wish chapter and for us, the application process was easy. We filled out an online form for Samuel with information about his diagnosis and the Lurie team's contact information. Once he was accepted, we were partnered with two wish granters. These ladies came to the house and had a conversation with Samuel about his favorite things, places, and activities.

They worked through his thoughts to come up with an ideal wish experience created just for him. The initial plan was for a trip to Disney Animation Studios in California to learn about being a "real artist." At that point in time he was constantly drawing and creating. The amount of regular old printer paper and various art supplies we went through on a weekly basis was insane!

The waiting list for that particular plan ended up being several months. In the interim, Samuel's gears shifted to a more animal-only mode. He talked about, drew, studied, and researched animals nonstop. We reached out to his wish granters and discussed the possibility of changing Samuel's wish to something more aligned with his passion at the time. They relayed the idea to their supervisor and devised another plan—this time a trip to the San Diego Zoo! As Samuel informed us, "It's the best zoo in the world, with 3,500 animals!"

Plans halted when COVID hit. A pause was put on all travel wishes, and we waited it out. As COVID mandates and limitations dragged on, the Make-A-Wish organization began encouraging families to consider coming up with an alternative wish idea that didn't involve travel or celebrity meet-and-greets. I explained this to Samuel and asked what else he might like his wish to be.

"A swimming pool!" he answered. Not a good plan, as he can't swim, and he doesn't like to be cold. I had also heard a rumor they don't grant pools for wishes, although I never confirmed that information. I explained my concerns with the pool idea, and he said, "I know! Mommy, when we're on vacation, I love to go in the hot tub with you. How about a hot tub?"

Bingo! What a fantastic idea! He does love a dip in a hot tub and some studies have shown that the warm water can do wonders to help soothe and relax the boys' muscles. We proposed that idea to our wish granters and they jumped on it, sought approval, and got things moving. They asked Samuel what he specifically hoped would be included as part of the hot tub wish and he said, "Enough room for our whole family (six of us), lights, and music!" They promised they would do the best they could to fulfill every aspect of his wish. We were responsible for making sure there was a safe and adequate spot for the hot tub to sit and that a proper electrical hookup was set up. From start to finish, the process with Make-A-Wish was about two and a half years total, due to all of those various delays and wish changes. (We have just recently begun the process for a wish for Josiah and are excited to see it come to fruition!)

Demolition day for the old parsonage came and went, and things began to move along. Daily progress seemed so very slow at times, yet there was a steady flow to the build. There were some delays, as is always to be expected, but forward momentum continued. The detail type decisions were fun: picking paint colors, choosing countertops, selecting flooring, and looking at light fixtures. It was so interesting to be included in the process, and we very much appreciated the amount of involvement we were able to have in it. Excitement built as we saw things happening. We looked forward to seeing what life would be like in our new home. [We were in the rental for almost exactly a year.]

The details of the build really don't seem that important, but I suppose in some ways they are. We ended up with a 5 bedroom/4 bathroom house. There are two bedrooms and a bathroom in the basement for Gabriel and Kaleigh, a master bedroom/bathroom for Cory and me, Jack and Jill style bedrooms with a shared accessible bathroom for Samuel and Josiah, and a spare "guest" bathroom in the hall. It's spacious and comfortable without being overwhelming. We chose glued down commercial grade LVP (Luxury Vinyl Plank) flooring. We ended up purchasing a 9 ft. table that seats 10 people—it has an X-style leg with a beam running underneath in the center. Doorways are 4 ft. wide throughout the house and a lever-style handle was chosen for ease of use. The center of light switches are at 3 1/2 ft. from the floor, perfectly usable by a standing adult and functional from a seated position as well. One side of the garage has a 9 ft. door, because many full-size accessible vehicles have a higher profile. The house has a nice open concept, and we've been very simple with the decor, somewhat modern farmhouse-ish. The floor plan included a large covered patio at the rear of the house, with adequate space for Samuel's hot tub. The hot tub came equipped with seating for seven (two of those seats are called "deep therapy seats" with extra massaging jets, they're amazing!), color changing lights, and a Bluetooth audio system. We can often be found "rockin' out" on the back patio in our swimsuits after a soak in the hot tub.

Since the house has been completed, we have had a couple of friends over who use wheelchairs full-time. They and their families agree that the decisions made by the committee on space, room orientation, and accessible features—like the microwave built into the island instead of on a counter or built into upper cabinets—were appropriate and necessary. We were very encouraged and pleased to hear their input.

While researching, I was in education mode. I gathered and

read and read some more. The facts and details and measurements and requirements for accessibility were necessary information I was learning. Yes, Duchenne was always on my mind, but usually only to the point that I needed those bits of information to be able to complete more research.

The ultimate goal of the committee in particular, and the church as a whole, was to build a house that would be functional for any family. Although we were to be the initial beneficiaries of this beautiful home, others down the road will be served by our congregation's incredible generosity. In theory, any combination of people could live here: a family with eight children would be able to fit, a spouse who has a stroke or other significant medical need would have the accessibility available, or a scenario in which someone's in-laws might need to move in could certainly work. Hopefully, this has been so well thought out that it will adequately house any number of future pastors' families for many, many years.

It was once we moved back in that the future reality hit me. I spoke before about the difficulty of daily Duchenne research. Up to that point, everything seemed so far in the future:

"When the boys are older…"

"At whatever point this is needed…"

"Down the road…"

Now it was real. It became personal.

"This is the table Josiah will maneuver his wheelchair up to for dinner."

"This is the bathroom where we will transfer Samuel to the toilet or the shower chair."

Despite the feelings of immense relief that the process was complete and the house was finished, a heavier sadness settled in for a bit.

I love our home. It's beautiful, comfortable, and by all reports exactly what the boys will eventually need. I'm still completely overwhelmed and extremely humbled by the generosity of so many people who have made this possible. We feel loved, supported, and so well-cared for.

God prepared our hearts to bring these boys into our family. He has blessed us with such a lovely and functional home. He has placed so many compassionate people right in front of us to care for our family in a multitude of ways. These are such amazing illustrations of God's love and provision for us in all things.

But those moments hit me every once in awhile—

I wish with all of my heart that we didn't need any of this.

I sorrow for what is to come and all the things the boys will have taken from them.

I worry about my ability to adequately care for them.

I think about further accommodations and changes that loom ahead.

I grieve the futures they won't get to have.

Here it is again, my companion: bittersweet moments, a paradox of joy and sadness. Happy moments tinged with the foreshadowing of what's to come. Duchenne is truly ever present.

Seven

The Day-to-Day

∽⚬⚭⚬∾

Our life on a daily basis is maybe not so different from other families, but then again, do I really know what other families do each day? Our own little brood is unique in many ways, but maybe there are more similarities to others than I realize.

How do things look for us? Honestly, our days are pretty simple, even though the overall family calendar appears to be crazy hectic. Cory, Gabriel (now 19), and Kaleigh (now 17) truly lead their own schedules. They are in and out and among us when they're free or on a weekend or an occasional evening (Cory more so than the other two). For the most part, it is Samuel and Josiah tagging along and hanging out with me, playing the role of my little ducklings.

Mornings are reasonably subdued. The boys get up rather early, usually between 6-6:30 am. They have some iPad time and are pretty quiet in the living room, allowing Cory and me to sleep just a little bit later. I get up and get my first cup of coffee and as long as the wind isn't howling or the temperature isn't less than about 35 degrees, I can be found outside sipping from my mug while checking email and Facebook and allowing my brain to begin to function just a smidge. Meanwhile, Cory gets breakfast prepped and the dishwasher emptied most days.

Gabriel moved out this last spring and lives in a duplex owned by my parents (long story there, but it's been vacant for years, so he asked them if he could move in). It's nice he's just four miles away, yet it allows him additional independence while attending community college and juggling work as an EMT/firefighter and time spent with his girlfriend, Grace. He's also not around in the mornings now to harass his brothers, which can make things a little easier for me, although we all certainly miss his sense of humor on a daily basis.

Since she bought her car, Kaleigh has lived her own independent schedule with reminders and check-ins, but has taken care of things for the most part on her own. She finished high school while working several part-time jobs and keeping up with her dance schedule. As of this writing (fall 2022), she has begun her freshman year at Hope College in Michigan, meeting new people and working part-time at a coffee shop. What a transition for her (and us!), but it's been a smooth one so far.

I try to get school done with at least one of the boys right after breakfast. On days we don't have PT, I can usually get both completed in the morning pretty easily. Josiah's schooling takes 45 minutes to an hour each day. Samuel's is usually done within about an hour to an hour and a half. They often listen in or sit near while the other is working with me, so Samuel gets some review of things, or Josiah learns about pinnipeds or how to split words into syllables, whatever Samuel happens to be working on at that time. In addition, we do so many extra "school-type" things: a monthly subscription to a kid's geography and culture kit, lots of reading, watching documentaries on TV, outings to the nature center at a local forest preserve, the zoo, and Chicago museums. They also learn a lot by simply being part of the household: making grocery lists, caring for our pets, learning how to show kindness and consideration to others. It's nonstop education, all the time, right? The boys are always so full of questions.

Two of our physical therapy days are a split schedule—one session, lunch break, then the other session. I actually prefer it that way. It makes for a long day, but we get the treat of ordering food out one day a week and packing for the other. On the other PT day, they have back-to-back sessions right after lunch. The variety keeps things from being too humdrum for any of us. On the split days we leave the house at 10:15 in the morning and don't return until 3 or 4 pm, depending on any errands I need to run. I figure I'm already in town three days a week, so I might as well save the time and gas money and run to the grocery store. We also end up with a little more than an hour at lunchtime between sessions to run a quick errand, explore something in the area, or just hang out at a playground for a bit.

We love to go on small adventures when the weather is even barely decent—a picnic, a new playground to try, a short hike at the state park, or a trip to the zoo. We have our favorite places and others we visit only occasionally. I'm always on the hunt for somewhere new to check out, but the boys and I also appreciate a bit of routine and repetition.

Once a week we typically go to Ruth's house for a potluck

style lunch (the same Ruth who is Leah's mom and the dance studio owner) with some other ladies I know. Several have kids and they all play while the adults get to chat. It's really nice most weeks, but sometimes behaviors get the best of my boys and it can be frustrating for me. I do look forward to the fellowship time with these friends when we can make it.

Gabriel is in and out from time to time for dinner or to hang out for a couple of hours, or he'll tag along for an errand if he's free. Kaleigh will join in when she's home for the occasional weekend or during school breaks.

The boys and I often have a little hot tub time in the middle of the afternoon or after dinner, especially on days when they have been walking a lot or we stopped at a playground for awhile. They do tell me that the water relaxes them, especially their leg muscles. They don't care to use it much in the heavy heat of summer, but once Illinois reaches a more moderate temperature, they are in it nearly daily, even through the winter.

We are very consistent with bedtime. We have found over time the boys will get up early, regardless of when we put them down. If we let them stay up later, they still get up early. If we put them to bed early, they may get up even earlier the next morning. We've discovered the magic window of time and we stick with it.

Many boys with Duchenne have trouble settling down for bed. Ours are no exception. After experimenting with timing shifts, TV vs. no screen time, a snack, changing up the bedtime routine, and them sometimes still being awake two hours after the intended bedtime, we decided to try melatonin. It has been a game changer for us. They take a little chewable tablet about thirty to forty-five minutes before bed and they're out within minutes of when we put them down—braces on, a hug, prayers, and nighty-night.

We have occasionally encountered others who I presume have Duchenne when we're out: the telltale enlarged calves, wheelchair-bound, sometimes the moon-shaped face (one of the potential side effects of steroid use), but I don't ever approach anyone. I wish I would, I wish I could, but here's why I don't, right or wrong:

We were in Myrtle Beach about seven years ago on vacation and went to an aquarium. Even at not quite 2 years old, Samuel was a budding animal expert. He was enthralled by everything we saw. In one of the exhibit areas, we came across a family with a teenage boy in a wheelchair. Cory and I had read and seen enough, even though Duchenne was relatively new to us, to feel confident that this young man had Duchenne. Wanting to acknowledge being a part of a shared world, a kinship, Cory stopped the father and asked if his son has Duchenne. The father's eyes briefly responded in recognition—someone had taken an interest, asked a question.

"Yes, he does, how did you know?"

Cory told him our young son also has Duchenne. Immediately the man's face changed and a sadness entered his eyes and his voice.

"I'm so very sorry."

That was all he said. No offer of hope or encouragement. No sage words of advice. Just a brief word of condolence and a look of empathy. I believe Cory had been hoping to make a connection, to share a personal bond with another father experiencing the same diagnosis. Obviously, that man's teenage son was much further along in the Duchenne timeline, and I can't pretend to know the hardships and grief and loss they had lived through to that point.

I'm hesitant to approach those I think may be similarly affected by Duchenne simply because of that encounter. It's not because it upset me, because truthfully, the discomfort I experienced was not for myself or our situation. Instead, I was worried that we perhaps exacerbated this father's sadness by inadvertently reminding him of what life must have been like when his son was young. He may have felt the effects of Duchenne were so far away. In those early years, he might have had hope that things would change medically and scientifically to prevent the decline his son was now experiencing.

I have since come across someone at the zoo, in an airport, in a mall, at a museum, and at a youth conference that I felt likely had Duchenne, but didn't speak to them. Again, I wish I would have. Duchenne can be very isolating, and although I'm often in a pretty good place, sometimes I'm not. I assume others must experience it similarly.

We have a hangtag for Samuel's medical stroller that explains a bit about Duchenne, and outlines some of the emergency protocols that might be helpful to first responders. I wonder if anyone will ever notice it and ask me questions. I'm happy to answer—I like to talk about my kids, even about the difficult stuff. When Samuel's medical scooter arrives (hopefully in the next few months), and later, when the boys reach the point of needing wheelchairs, I plan to purchase Duchenne bumper stickers (or better yet, have them custom made) encouraging people to ask questions.

We also have some business cards provided by PPMD that say: "You've just met someone with Duchenne Muscular Dystrophy. Thank you for your interest…" I keep a few in my wallet for the day that I might be approached by someone asking questions out of curiosity or, similar to Cory, wanting to simply make a connection.

I didn't yet have those cards when just such an opportunity arose. I was at Costco a couple of years ago, and Samuel was still pretty little. His calves have had an obvious enlargement since he was rather young. It was summer, and he was wearing shorts. I had just taken him to the bathroom, and a stranger stopped me and said something like "Boy, look at those calves! Does he play soccer? Wrestling?"

I was in a really good frame of mind at that time and simply used the interest taken in my son as an opportunity to educate. I chose my words carefully and spoke in a rather matter-of-fact way, but still feel I may have made this gentleman uncomfortable. Although I skimmed the surface and didn't go into detail about life expectancy and all that nonsense, he realized the scenario was much more serious than he could have imagined when he asked the innocuous question.

I've had similar opportunities several other times. It's always a comment on the calves—and I usually say about the same thing: "He has Duchenne Muscular Dystrophy, the enlargement you see in the calves is actually muscle fiber that has broken down and been replaced by fatty tissue."

Simple and to the point. A few people have uttered an apology and said they would pray for our family. Others have shown genuine interest and asked a few follow-up questions. Again, I'm usually more than happy to talk about my kids for many reasons, but especially in this area, I feel well-versed enough to have an in-depth conversation if someone is interested.

Going to physical therapy three times a week when we live 30 minutes away certainly adds up the mileage and the time spent surrounding the whole "PT experience." Of course, we miss some sessions here and there due to illness, vacation, or where holidays fall. This is yet another reason homeschooling has been such a wonderful choice for our family. I don't know how we would even be able to consider fitting this into our day if we didn't homeschool. However, we also know the benefits of physical therapy for the boys far outweigh any minor inconveniences. Many days I'm able to get some exercise by pushing one of the boys in a stroller while the other is in their session, and then I swap them out and walk some more. On days when the weather is cruddy, they get extra iPad time and I catch up on emails on my phone or read a book. A rough estimate would be around 6,500 miles driven a year for physical therapy and 550+ hours dedicated to that task. No wonder I try to run errands while we're already in town!

I've mentioned before that Cory works long hours. He has his regular commitment as pastor of a congregation and all the things that come along with that. He additionally does some work for this particular district of our church denomination as a regional vice president. He volunteers with Meals on Wheels a couple of times a month and sometimes serves breakfast at the homeless shelter in our county. He occasionally participates in a local theater group and loves his weekly Adult Tap class. His daily schedule, however, is sometimes flexible enough to allow him to accompany us on some of those field trips, or take the dog to the vet or groomer so I don't have to haul the boys with me to do so. He misses lots of dinners and bedtimes due to evening commitments, but is semi-regularly able to spend an hour or two with the kids in the afternoon. Sometimes they go to the dog park with our pup, Winnie. Other times they'll grab an ice cream treat. As previously mentioned, he also nearly always takes care of the breakfast routine with Samuel and Josiah.

The dynamic between the big kids and little kids has worked really well in so many ways over these years. Gabriel and Kaleigh have learned some serious parenting skills as we occasionally used them as built-in babysitters. They were also active participants in feeding bottles, changing diapers, and playing with the boys, even when not on babysitter duty. The kids all have a really good relationship despite their age difference. Truly one of the most difficult things as far as all-six-of-us-together-family-time has been finding activities and events that interest all of us, but we've managed: the zoo, Indiana Beach (amusement park not too far from where we live), the Museum of Science and Industry, an indoor water park, local parks, farmers' markets, and festivals have all been good choices that appeal in some way to each of us.

With neither Gabriel or Kaleigh living at home full time anymore, additional changes arrived for us over a period of just a few short months. I'm so proud of their level of independence and confidence, but I also really appreciate the phone calls or FaceTimes with me when there are questions, or seeking a brief bit of advice, or even just wanting to include me in their day.

The boys have adjusted pretty well to them being gone. Things seem a tiny bit less chaotic and a little more quiet on a day-to-day basis, which seems certainly both good and bad to me! We're finding our way.

Eight

Telling the Boys

There have been many times I hear questions like, "What do the boys know about their diagnosis?" or "How do you decide what to tell them?" This is something so individualized to each family, but I can tell you what we've done and how it seems to have gone so far.

Duchenne and adoption: both MAJOR topics. Knowing when to reveal information can be a burden of its own, but being secretive or waiting too long can be hurtful, upsetting, or damaging. We decided from the beginning to not hide anything from the boys. We wanted to answer questions honestly and openly when they came up, and planned to share age appropriate information with the two of them as things move along.

I don't remember the first time Samuel specifically asked about adoption or his "other family." Adoption has always just been a part of our family's vocabulary with him. We are careful to never speak negatively about his birth family. We tell him simply that they were not able to take care of him and they made the decision to have us adopt him and he is our son. It certainly helps that we have several friends who have also adopted children. This doesn't seem weird or out of the ordinary to Samuel and Josiah—it's just another way people have kids.

We enrolled Samuel in 3-year-old preschool at the same parochial school the big kids attended for years. The many ways that didn't work for him is a story all its own. However, one day on the way to school, he asked me about Gabriel and Kaleigh:

Samuel: Gabriel and Kaleigh were in your tummy, right mommy?

Me: Yes, they were.

S: I was in another lady's tummy, right?

Me: Yes, Samuel, and that lady decided to ask us to take care of you and love you and have you be our son.

S: I went to the zoo lots of times when I was living with that other family. (Not true, as he was only in the temporary home for seven weeks, and besides, how could he possibly even remember?)

Me: I don't know, maybe you did. But I do know you go to the zoo lots of times with us.

S: I like the zoo….So, the men that work on the power lines have to wear special boots and gloves so the electricity doesn't get them?

Just like that, the conversation shifted. He didn't hardly bat an eyelash. I can't comment on the number of times he has taken things like that in stride, or explained things in his own way to Josiah. Adoption has never been a specific regular topic of conversation, but again, just part of the vocabulary of our household.

The word "Duchenne" has been pretty much the same scenario. They hear us talking to other people. They know that they go to PT and not all kids do. They are well aware of the fact that most other people don't wear splints on their legs at night. Samuel knows that his medical stroller was purchased through our insurance and he sees other kids his age totally having outgrown a stroller of any sort. We recently ordered a medical scooter for him to use for long distances/lengthy outings, certainly not the norm for an 8 year old.

There was another time very recently, when some friends, Frank and Sue, offered to host a kick-off fundraiser working toward some savings for the eventual purchase of an accessible van. Frank is the lead singer of a band and they held the event at a local pub. We decided selling T-shirts as an ongoing fundraiser in addition could be a good idea and someone suggested Samuel should be the artist/designer. I asked him to draw a picture for the shirt front but didn't explain to him beyond saying something like, "It's to raise money to start saving up for the cost of a van we're going to need someday." His picture is a van with he and Josiah standing outside of it. It's pretty simple, but I think it's perfect.

Josiah asked what he was drawing and Samuel said, "I'm making a picture for a T-shirt for our fundraiser. The band is going to play, and people are going to come, and we're going to raise money to get us a van that wheelchairs can go in. Because someday, Josiah, we're going to need wheelchairs."

Just like that again, in a completely matter-of-fact way. I was blown away. I know for a FACT that no one has ever directly told him about their future wheelchair needs. One of the families we know has a 17-year-old son who has Duchenne, and he uses a wheelchair full-time. They came to dinner once, that's it. Did he make the connection then? And Josiah? When Samuel told him about this project, he said, "Oh, OK," and moved on with his day.

That first fundraiser was called Workin' for Wheels. It was such a fun time, with music and food and raffle baskets. We greatly appreciated being approached by these friends in order to get some fundraising started. They know how much money we might be talking about when thinking of a vehicle that would adequately transport two power wheelchairs (We received an initial quote of around $70,000 for an accessible Ford Transit that will hold the weight of two powerchairs and allow for a couple of other passengers. Although, in theory, we won't need such a vehicle for hopefully three to five more years, that's certainly a lot of money to plan for and work toward.). We didn't have to do a thing except show up for the event. It was humbling again to see the community we live in come together in support of us, and in such a fun way!

We met Val at that fundraiser. Her family has also been touched by Duchenne (a brother, two cousins, and an uncle) and she lives in a neighboring town. That night she told me she had an idea for another fundraiser but didn't want to overwhelm me. We exchanged numbers with the promise to reach out soon to talk about her thoughts. A few months later we attended her event which she named Cuttin' for Wheels. Val owns a hair salon and partnered with another salon in the area to offer free haircuts for a donation. But beyond that, she secured many raffle baskets and again sold T-shirts. She arranged for a pop-up coffee shop and a BBQ stand to be in attendance. Both of those businesses also offered a portion of their profits to the cause. We saw many familiar faces as we spent the afternoon amid the excitement of all the activity going on. We also saw many new faces, people simply interested in being a part of this event to help our family and to support our sons. There I was, thankful and humbled all over again. Cuttin' for Wheels was also a huge success.

There have been discussions with Val and Sue and a few others about some ideas for additional fundraising in the future because we're still a long way from reaching even a portion of that financial goal. We will see how this all plays out over the next few years. Each time these immense kindnesses have been shown to us, we are at first a little surprised at the generosity of others, and then just so appreciative of the love shown to us. Don't let anyone tell you there's not good in this world, we've been on the receiving end of so much of that good!

Samuel has gotten used to people noticing his legs. A gentleman stopped me at the greenhouse recently. "Excuse me, is that your son? I'm just curious how his calves could be so muscular so young." Here we go…I gave the typical response of fatty, fibrous tissue replacing healthy muscle as it breaks down. He said he'd pray for our family and that was that. Samuel then told me he knows lots of times when people have stopped and asked if he runs track or plays soccer. Again, he's not emotional or upset, just stating truth as he knows it. He's very much like a sage old man about it.

Sometimes Samuel will say things like, "Josiah, because we have muscular dystrophy, you know that means our muscles work differently. It means we can get more tired. It means we might need to take a break and rest. It means we might get to watch a little more TV or have more iPad time."

All of this is true. Because Samuel is so calm, cool, and collected about these things and says them with no distress or upset, Josiah seems to follow suit. He has an awful lot of trust in his older brother, and I firmly believe he knows he really won't be led astray. What Samuel says is fact, and Josiah usually accepts it. However, Josiah will sometimes say things like, "Samuel, maybe some day you'll be in a wheelchair, but I'll be in my combine, dancing with a disco ball!" Josiah's personality is so very interesting, a crazy combination of serious and goofball.

Samuel has always been really good about self-monitoring his energy level. He'll take breaks when needed. Often, at a playground, he'll come over and sit by me for a bit while Josiah keeps climbing and running and playing. "Mommy, it must be nice to be young and have so much energy." (Remember, there's just a 21 month difference between these two!) Sometimes, he'll plant himself at the top of the play structure and be the pirate captain, barking out orders, which of course, Josiah dutifully follows (at least some of the time).

Josiah has not been nearly as adept at keeping his activity in check and taking breaks. He is go, go, go, go nearly all the time. As he's getting a bit older and the effects of Duchenne are seen a little more readily, it's fallen on us as parents to push him to drink a little more water, to require him to sit and rest for a bit, to strongly encourage him to accept a stroller ride now and again. He's getting a bit better about figuring out what his body needs, and he's starting to take more cues from Samuel in that regard.

The boys both know the words "Duchenne Muscular Dystrophy" and they know their muscles work differently, that they get tired a little more easily, they aren't really supposed to jump in bounce houses or climb the stairs. At this point they DON'T know that they will lose more and more strength and that we will eventually have to do basically everything for them (at least I don't think they do?). Although they both usually acknowledge that there will be a wheelchair in their future, I don't believe the connection has really been made yet about what that wheelchair really means for their daily experiences. They don't understand that they won't be able to dress themselves. They don't comprehend that I will again be brushing their teeth as I did when they were itty bitty boys. They haven't put the pieces together that we will be feeding them when they can no longer feed themselves. They don't have a clue that their expected lifespan is so much shorter than everyone else in our household.

We've made a point to not be overly emotional about changes that have happened up to this point. We have been honest and open and shared information with the boys as we feel appropriate for their age and maturity. Josiah, of course, observes things happening sooner for Samuel. As changes have happened for Josiah, the transitions seem to have been made a little bit easier. He observes those gradual changes happening for Samuel and seems to understand, or at least accept, that those same changes will happen for him in time.

I believe it has also made some difference that Gabriel and Kaleigh are so much older. There are zero comparisons made by the boys to their older siblings. Just like typical siblings who are close in age, the comparison and competition is with each other, and there certainly is plenty of that!

We don't have a particular game plan about how we will continue this dialogue with the boys as things progress. There will be some hard conversations, difficult realizations, multiple adjustments, and numerous accommodations made. We intend to do our best to hit them head on and with honesty and frank, open discussions when the boys seem ready and able to hear that information, just like we've begun. We will continue to educate others as best we can and advocate for the boys when needed.

There are so many changes for them in the future. So many losses. I hope that they both are able to continually just take it in stride. I hope that I am able to be thankful for every day that I get to have with them. I hope that I am able to serve and love and assist them in every need. I hope that God provides me with the physical, mental, and emotional strength to continue along this journey we've begun. I pray we can give the boys things to look forward to and a life full of love, with adventures both big and small.

Nine

My Journey Beyond Grief

⟡

This book is mostly about my little guys and how all the things we've lived through had to happen in order to get the two of them to us to complete our family. I hope it paints a picture of how God has woven the beautifully orchestrated pieces of our lives together to this point in time. This book is about finding joy and hope and living life despite the grief continually hanging out in the background. But part of the story is also about me: as mom, as caregiver, and as author (It seems so weird to say that!).

I wonder if some of the moments I've shared, the glimpses I've given, have left a few questions...like the questions I'm so often asked by others as I've told bits and pieces of our family's story in the midst of a casual conversation.

"Is it hard for you to talk about your boys? About your life?"

"How did you and Cory meet? You were pretty young, right?"

"What led you to the foster care/adoption route in the first place? Why didn't you just plan to have more biological children? Did it have to do with your first pregnancy loss and the complications with Gabriel's birth?"

"When did you find out Gabriel had a hearing loss?"

"You said you served as foster parents for a brief time and then took a pause. Did something happen to then lead you toward infant adoption instead?"

"Is your adoption timeline and the cost you incurred typical?"

"I heard you ran a marathon; what was that experience like?"

"Your boys were able to continue in-person PT during COVID, what DID change for you? How did you and your family cope during that time?"

"How do you personally deal with stress and the busyness of the family schedule? What do you do to work through the grief and loss you experience now and what you know is to come?"

I've struggled for many years with really finding my place: a daughter, an excellent student, a reliable worker, a musician with adequate skill, a speech therapist, a pastor's wife, a mom, and a teacher. Where do I fit? High achievement coupled with a lack of confidence, shyness, awkwardness, and a discomfort with social situations have often made it hard for me to feel like I really fit in much of anywhere. I've served in all those roles reasonably well, and along the way have found additional pieces of myself that I liked, others that I didn't.

It hasn't been until the last five to seven years that I really have grown comfortable with who I am. The need to people please has been reduced. The Type-A-ness of me has relaxed just a bit. I'm confident (but still very, very frustrated at times) about parenting. I know which people in our circle genuinely care, provide support, and love me and my family wholeheartedly. I know who I can trust to not judge on my angry, grumpy, tired, and complaint-filled days. I know who will celebrate with me in triumphs, large and small. I enjoy genuine conversation and greatly appreciate a sense of humor in others. For the most part, I've settled into a general contentment in my days, much more willingness to share emotion, and a general openness about life and my experiences.

Letting people in to my hurts and even my joys has been foreign since I was little. I've never been super emotional about things. I've been embarrassed easily by "letting go" and showing those pieces of me. I didn't dare let people see me cry.

I was raised in a very private household. We just didn't share about situations that were perceived to be our business or our trouble with others openly. I have always had a hard time asking for help or sharing my sadness with others. I have often not wanted to talk about the bad things. I am more apt to spend time mulling things over in my head, seeking options to come to a solution, and trying to fix it solo.

On the other end of things, I think some of my shyness also kept me from wanting much outward praise when I achieved something important. I believe I have always had a hard time accepting genuine compliments from people because of that. I feel an inner sense of pride for a job well done, but have never wanted to be the center of attention or applauded in a big way.

Cory and I met our third day of college our freshman year at Ball State University at a "welcome picnic" put on by the Lutheran student group. We became friends immediately and hung out a lot in a fun group of 8-10 others. We started dating at the beginning of our second semester and got married right after finishing college (Cory with a bachelor's degree in music education and me six months later with a master's degrees in speech-language pathology). I found a comfort and safety with Cory and discovered some of those pieces of myself as we began to figure out how the two of us fit together.

We moved after college and began working in our respective careers. A couple of years later we began planning to start a family. The enormity of losing our first pregnancy at 20 weeks was something that now seems so far in the distant past that I often have a hard time remembering just how heavy a chapter it was. Every once in a while bits of memory pass by from the brief time in the hospital or once we were back home without her, and it hits me to the core.

When those scenes flash before me, I'm right back in that sadness and there is a weight to my spirit. There was never truly an explanation as to why we made it to 20 weeks and no further—some speculation, but no diagnosis. This added to the fear and worry during my other two pregnancies. Of course, I was always wondering in the background of my consciousness if it would happen again. We named our daughter, Caitlyn, and although we don't talk about her much, all four of our other kids know about their "older" sister.

My pregnancy with Gabriel was naturally fraught with concern and some anxiety. We were carefully monitored and in good hands, but that didn't entirely relieve the stress. The pregnancy was rather unremarkable, but it was the delivery that was traumatic in many ways. I was induced a couple of weeks early because the doctors were estimating him to be a pretty big baby. Labor itself was extremely painful because the effects of the epidural pooled to one side of my body and I was feeling every bit of the contractions on the other side. Delivery was difficult, and without going into graphic detail, let's just say he ended up with a broken collar bone, and I lost so much blood—passing out as a result—that I required a transfusion.

As already crazy as all of that felt, what a huge blessing it was that his collar bone was fractured during delivery. We called in the lactation consultant because he was having trouble nursing. She saw his arm looked a little funny, so sent him to the nursery to be checked out. It was then that they discovered the break. While there, the nurses also realized he was having trouble regulating his temperature. The end result was a group B strep infection (even though my culture had been negative when tested as part of the pregnancy protocol).

Gabriel entered the NICU as a very, very sick baby. The infection led to sepsis, and he ended up on a ventilator as well. Each day that passed seemed like more and more difficult news to bear. A corner was turned at around 10 days old, and after 16 days in the NICU, he was able to come home with us. High dose antibiotics saved his life, but we also fully believe they caused his permanent hearing loss.

The pregnancy and delivery with Kaleigh were truly un-remarkable. There was still this underlying concern that something would go wrong. Of course it would. Why wouldn't it? Those fears proved to be unnecessary, and a sweet baby girl came home with us the day before Christmas. Gabriel's world as an almost 2 year old was turned upside down, but he got used to her being around pretty quickly.

Cory graduated from seminary and we moved to Illinois to the church I've previously spoken so fondly about. Having grown up in the suburbs of Indianapolis, it was a big change for me to be thirty minutes from "town." A couple of restaurants and a few small stores exist out where we live, but the bulk of our shopping and errand-running requires a drive.

I wasn't sure how I would settle in to country living, but it didn't take long at all for me to realize how peaceful and amazing it is. I believe it was the weekend we moved in that I was sitting upstairs in Kaleigh's room with the windows open (she was 6 months old at the time). I heard owls hooting back and forth, and all I could do was smile as I listened, rocking her forward and back. I discovered very quickly, that for me, we were in the perfect place: the quiet and beauty of the country, with Target and restaurants and all those other conveniences 30 minutes away, and the cultural opportunities of the big city (Chicago) just an hour from our new home.

We settled in well and the kids grew. We didn't actually discover Gabriel's hearing loss until he was four. He failed the newborn screening at the hospital before being discharged from the NICU, which is not uncommon. He then passed an evaluation a little later with a pediatric audiologist, and he didn't act in any way as if he might have a hearing loss. He responded appropriately in different environments and never asked for the volume to be turned up on the TV. He was a late talker, but understood everything we said, following two and three step directions with ease. We taught him some sign language to help avoid frustration with getting across his needs and wants. In fact, he learned over 200 signs in a matter of a couple of months.

At a little over 2 years old, Gabriel had a language explosion, so we really never had any suspicions that his hearing was anything but perfect. He did fail a hearing screening in three-year-old preschool, but we were told they were convinced he didn't understand the instructions and we all dismissed it at the time. He failed the screening again in four-year-old preschool and was referred for an evaluation. It was then discovered that the little guy had learned how to read lips to supplement his hearing deficit. He was functioning at a nearly normal level even though the results of the audiogram indicated a moderate-to-severe hearing loss. He was fitted with hearing aids within weeks. When we left the audiologist's office with them in for the first time, he said, "Mommy, I can hear the wind blowing the leaves in the trees. I never heard that before." We never knew how much he was missing.

Our new life in Illinois was busy with learning and playing and adventuring. When Kaleigh was 3 years old, we decided we'd like to grow our family again. My pregnancies were filled with enough worry and concern that we thought adoption could be a better plan. Cory and I had often talked about wanting to adopt some day even way back when we were first dating.

After a little research, we determined traditional infant adoption seemed too expensive and the travel requirements for international adoption would be too large a burden with our other children at home. So, we opted to become licensed foster parents. Our plan was to be open to caring for a child/children for the time they needed us, and if it turned into an adoption possibility, then all the better.

What a disaster fostering turned out to be for us! We completed our training, all the while being told that there is such a HUGE need for foster parents. Once we finished the licensing process, it was shared with us in more detail that a radius around the child's home address is looked at for placements, ideally keeping them in their home school district.

This became problematic because of our rural setting, and therefore not a large need for foster parents in the immediate area. Placements did occur outside of that radius, but they were nearly always unusual circumstances. These unusual circumstances were the kind of phone calls we received: a sibling group of five (our license didn't even cover seven total children in the home), a pregnant teen nearing delivery (our two children were 7 and 5 years old at the time, and we honestly weren't in a place in our lives to adequately parent a teen at all, let alone one about to have a baby), a teen who had run away from home (not equipped for that either), a teen who had attempted suicide multiple times (ummm, not equipped).

We had read quite a bit about not disrupting birth order when fostering/adopting, so ideally were hoping for a child or children under 5 years old. Months of waiting and the only phone calls we received were for those types of placements mentioned above that we felt we couldn't possibly accept. We finally received a call about an 8-year-old boy, Michael, and his 18-month-old half brother, Jacob (names have been changed). The caseworker gave us some basic information about some educational and behavioral needs for the older sibling, but assured us he could be enrolled in a regular classroom with some resource help. Because the older boy was just about Gabriel's age, and the younger was clearly quite a bit younger than Kaleigh, we agreed to their placement and they were brought to our home a day or two later.

It was only after the placement occurred that we found out that indeed, Michael's behaviors and educational needs required a specialized behavioral management classroom (Our local school district did not have such a thing, so we connected with a neighboring district about enrolling there.). We were informed that he also was bipolar and on heavy duty medication and was scheduled for weekly appointments with a psychiatrist an hour from our house. Oh, and by the way, we were their fifth foster home since the little guy was born—keep in mind he was only 18 months old when they came to us. So many things should have been openly shared with us so we could have made an educated decision to accept or opt out of this particular placement. We had asked questions...several questions...direct questions...yet none of this pertinent information was provided to us.

We felt blindsided. Of course, an adjustment period was expected. We never assumed everything would go smoothly. We had planned and prepped for additional children to join our family, bringing with them their own personalities and experiences. However, we were NOT prepared for this particular situation in the slightest.

The neighboring school district fought us about needing to re-test and develop a new IEP prior to enrolling Michael in school, even though he came to us with a perfectly valid IEP and should not have been denied enrollment. It took a week to get him enrolled in school under duress. We had to push the foster care agency for transportation to the psychiatric appointments, because the days and times the appointments were already scheduled were not feasible for us to manage.

There were violent outbursts so aggressive that I feared for the other children's safety. Michael ripped down the curtain rod, picked up and threw the piano bench at me, and on and on and on. We reached out for help immediately and were told that because we weren't "crisis trained" we were not allowed to touch him, not even to hold him tight so that he or someone else couldn't get hurt. What could we do? We were instructed to follow him around with a notebook, listing events. So I did. He dumped the markers on the floor and threw the tin across the room, screamed in a rage while tearing all of the clothes off the hangers, hit me and kicked me and spat at me in addition to the aforementioned piano bench throwing and pulling down the curtain rod. Each time these episodes started, I'd scream for Gabriel and Kaleigh to go upstairs to the safety of their bedrooms, and I positioned myself between Michael and his little brother. Cory helped when and how he could, maintaining a full-time job and navigating things at home with me as best as possible at the time.

Gabriel and Kaleigh were frightened. They didn't want to say or do anything that might set Michael off. At the same time, they were little kids trying to be friendly and welcoming to this new guest in our home, and they didn't have a clue as to what to do when this kind of scenario was presented.

I was on edge and a nervous wreck, never knowing what Michael might do, trying to anticipate every move, while also maintaining the normal household routine and raise three other children. Over the course of two weeks I lost 12 pounds. I wasn't sleeping well, I wasn't able to take the time to eat because someone always needed something or I was dealing with another outburst/crisis, and the stress, oh my goodness, the stress.

Up to this point, Michael's violence had been toward inanimate objects (several things broken beyond repair) and me. He didn't seem to dare think about striking out physically to Cory, although I believe there was one time he did spit at him. Michael had also gotten in trouble at school in those first few days for overturning several desks in a rage and physically attacking the principal.

The final straw was one afternoon when Michael started up and I hollered to Gabriel and Kaleigh to go upstairs. Before I could get between him and his little brother, or get Jacob picked up and in my arms, Michael had a horrifying look of rage on his face and made guttural animal-like sounds. He ran to Jacob and knocked him flat on his back. Jacob looked stunned—the wind knocked out of him. I scooped him up and knew in that moment I couldn't take any more. This was not in any way what we signed up for, and we didn't know how to help or what to do to change any of it. Michael needed much more than we could offer.

Cory called the agency immediately, and they considered having Michael committed to the psychiatric ward. However, there were no open beds at the time, couldn't we keep him a few more days? Cory replied that none of this was a surprise to any of them, they knew Michael's history, we'd been updating them on the behaviors throughout the two weeks since he'd moved in with us. We had reached the end of what we were able to manage (we weren't "managing" at all, more like barely surviving), but because it was already evening, we would allow him to stay one more night in order for them to find another placement.

I sent Michael to school the next morning. While he was gone, I packed up his meager belongings. They did find another home for him, and it was arranged for a social worker to come to our house to meet him when he got off the bus. She simply told him that he wouldn't be living here any more and she was going to take him to another house. He didn't react at all. He didn't question what was going to happen to his brother. He didn't ask to stay or apologize for his behaviors. He simply said "OK" and got in the car with her. Wow.

We were hoping to keep Jacob in our home, and we told the caseworkers our openness to him staying as long as he needed. When he came to us, he was basically nonverbal, nodding his head, pointing, and grunting to get his point across. The moment Michael was out of our house, Jacob came alive. He giggled and smiled and his little personality emerged. We started teaching him some signs. He was engaged and interested in us and in the world and he started speaking some words.

About two weeks later, we got a call that the decision was made to move Jacob to where Michael was living. Again, wow. That news struck me. This little guy, although yes, a half sibling to Michael, didn't have a relationship with him. Michael didn't interact with or treat him like a brother. He didn't engage with Jacob basically at all. However, keeping siblings together is of utmost importance much of the time in foster care. I get it. But again, I don't. Shouldn't individual circumstances be taken into consideration? We had a day or two to also get his few belongings together and sent him on his way.

We've not seen either of them again. I have prayed for these many years that all is well. I wonder if Michael got the additional help/therapy/medication and behavioral and educational services he needed. I want to believe Jacob continued to thrive and is flourishing in school and in life. I hope my gut is wrong about what things seemed to potentially look like for them moving forward when each of them left our home.

A little while later we were offered the opportunity to serve as a respite family for a 10-month-old boy. In this particular instance, the family had previously planned a vacation and were not planning to take the baby with them. We took him in for about a week. There were a couple more phone calls about situations that again didn't seem appropriate with two small children in the house (a pair of sibling teens, another large family group). An additional few months passed and we decided that maybe foster care was not the path we were meant to be continuing.

That's when the opportunity to teach preschool at my children's school came about, so we put fostering on hold and I accepted the job. I taught three days a week for two years. The staff I worked with at the time was phenomenal: loving, kind, genuinely good people, not to mention really, really good at their jobs. I certainly used bits and pieces of my previous speech pathology knowledge to help a few little ones with their articulation concerns, but the training and experience I've had as a parent of small children prepared me to a much larger degree for this job.

If imitation is the sincerest form of flattery, then I flattered a lot of other teachers. I found forums and groups to borrow ideas from and adapted numerous crafts and activities to suit my needs. I used every bit of creative muscle in me and I had so much fun. A classroom of interested and excited 4-year-old students is the best. Not every day was easy, and I put a lot of extra time into the preparation and planning outside of actual school hours, but I think back on those two years with a great fondness. Teaching sixteen of those little ones at a time is certainly exhausting, but the amount of learning that occurred and the number of giant squishy hugs I got daily were both amazing and wonderful.

Back in our home, we engaged in another series of conversations about how best to move forward to grow our family. Were we content with the way things were? Were we open to considering other options? Did Cory and I both still feel the pull to add to our family? More research, phone calls, an interview, a contract signed, and we ended up entering the world of infant adoption.

We felt so very hopeful at the beginning. The number of waiting families when compared to the number of adoptions per year with this particular agency at that time averaged out to a likely 12- to 18-month wait time. Over the course of our first two-year contract, the agency accepted more and more prospective adoptive parents, yet their number of average monthly placements remained the same. Our profile was presented time and time again. They assured us that all was well, and we just needed to be patient, because the process will work. Over time, we became increasingly disappointed in the quality of service we were provided, and we were not in favor of some of the changes to their business practices. However, we felt kind of stuck. We had already invested a hefty chunk of cash and felt it would be difficult to start over with another agency from scratch.

Once that initial two-year contract expired, we re-signed for six more months, and then six more months, and then six more months, and then six more months. Each time we were told "It's bound to happen any day," "Your patience will pay off," "It's only another six months." Each time we wrote a check, we went further and further into debt to try to make this happen. [News about Samuel came from an outside source anyway, but we do feel that at least our experiences with that agency, good or bad, led us now to have been able to advise/counsel several other couples we know about our personal experience. No two adoption stories are the same, but we are happy to share ours.]

After Samuel was home with us, we became serious about

kicking our debt's booty (the $25,000 during the four years of waiting —although not all of that was borrowed, some we were able to pay out of pocket at the time, plus approximately $10,000 more we borrowed for Samuel's placement. The total money we spent is a lot, but not out of range.). We took on a daily paper route to add just enough income to pay off what we had borrowed from our parents for adoption expenses. I took care of the weekday route and Cory handled the weekend delivery. Some days I could get the route completed before picking the big kids up from school during the last couple of months they attended. On other days, when I didn't get quite finished, they helped roll and rubber band the papers while I drove to complete the route. Samuel took his afternoon nap while we listened to "The Dave Ramsey Show" each of those afternoons. It did a lot to help motivate me to keep working towards being debt free. It took about a year to be able to pay off the last of our borrowed funds for Samuel's adoption.

Josiah's adoption didn't involve us borrowing as much money. The bulk of the previous total borrowed had been the contract fee for advertising and facilitating connections at that first agency. Josiah's adoption, like Samuel's, through the social service agency, required a placement fee and the amount set by the attorney to file paperwork for us. With his entrance to our family being a rather big surprise in a very short period of time, we also didn't have money set aside to pay those fees. We were able to borrow approximately $8,000 from our parents again. We paid that back in a matter of months. We also applied for and were awarded an adoption grant for each of the boys' adoptions (about $3,000).

Time passed and our day-to-day settled in to a comfortable routine. Once we committed to training for that first 8K run with Parent Project Muscular Dystrophy, we decided it was time to share the boys' diagnosis.

There had been a time previously when I announced to Cory I wanted to be able to run a 5K. I didn't feel I needed a race to prove anything. I just wanted to be able to say I could do it. I started a training plan and over about eight weeks I went from a complete non-runner to being able to finish that 3.1 miles without stopping. The summer temps hit hard that year and exceedingly high heat and humidity weighed heavily on me. We went on vacation, and it was equally as hot and humid. I took some time off…too much time off, and didn't return to it when the weather became more bearable.

Several years later we were offered the opportunity to run the Shamrock Shuffle for PPMD. That became the beginning of my serious running journey. Always the organized planner, I followed a training plan again and was able to accomplish the task. The monotony of continually lapping the same .10 mile track at the gym eventually bored me. It was spring, so I tried some outside running. I discovered I loved running outdoors. I eventually was able to handle a wide range of temperatures, and I figured out how to best dress for the weather of the day. The freedom of open space and the quiet of the country roads brought a lot of peace to a sometimes troubled spirit.

Following the Shamrock Shuffle, I thought I should maybe try a 10K. That, too, was successful and really kind of fun. I liked the T-shirts. I liked the "bling." I liked the anticipation of the event at the start line and the camaraderie felt once the tightly packed group thinned out and I found myself running alongside other people journeying at my pace, all of us with the same overall goal.

After a smattering of shorter races, I thought to myself, "What next?" Naturally, a half marathon. I was feeling strong and healthy. I had lost a little weight and toned up some. I felt great! I received other enormous benefits from running as well. I've always been pretty high energy, a bit of a worrier, and on the go so much of the time. I found that on days I went for a run, long or short (but especially long), I was more relaxed and mellow. I wasn't exhausted and drained for the day, but just tired enough to "take the edge off." The best kind of tired!

I had another goal, followed another training plan, and completed another successful race. My half marathon goal time was 2 hours and 10 minutes. I finished the race in 2 hours, 10 minutes, and 19 seconds. I'd call that a win!

I registered for more races after that, a mixture of shorter and longer, sometimes with Cory and/or friends, other times solo. I recruited another set of teammates to participate in the Rock 'n' Roll Half Marathon and 5K, also benefiting PPMD. We again received enormous support and had a great time planning and running. It rained throughout the entire course for the half marathon, which was a first for me. I typically make a beeline for home at the first drops of precipitation during a training run. It was a warm rain, not coming down too hard, and it actually felt amazing. I had my trusted running hat on and the brim of it kept the rain out of my face. This particular run was held in the middle of July and could have had disastrously hot temperatures and been an entirely miserable experience. However, it was about the best run I've ever had, especially at that distance. Squishy shoes and the disgusting feet to deal with afterward were certainly a reality after running in water for 13.1 miles, but it was a wonderful day nonetheless.

Over time several people asked me about my intentions to attempt a longer distance. My answer was always something like, "A half marathon is plenty far enough for me. Who needs a marathon? I'm good." However, there was a thought percolating in my brain. I wanted to ignore it, but my planning nature got the best of me. What next? Well, yes, a marathon, right? Wouldn't it be an incredible thing to have a marathon on my bucket list? I was able to ignore it for awhile, but finally decided that yes, I wanted to run a marathon before my 45th birthday. So, I did it. In October 2019, I signed up to be a charity runner (again with PPMD) for the Chicago Marathon for October 2020. The run was to be held seven months before my 45th birthday.

Because nothing is truly official until it's "Facebook Official," I posted that I had made that leap and was gonna try this really big thing. I invited any and all of the other crazy people in my life to join me for this journey. I got one taker. My dear friend, Anne, who has herself become a bit of a fitness nut over the last several years, was game to try it. We have been friends for over 35 years, but now we are also BRFs (Best Running Friends).

Here's where that dreaded "C" word comes in again, COVID. We all know what happened in March 2020. The entire world shut down. Anne and I waited for months to see what would happen with the marathon. Would it go on as scheduled? Would it be postponed? Would this new "virtual" option for everything under the sun be the way they held it that year? Anne and I kept plugging away at the training plan, making steady progress, and sharing daily updates about our runs, about our days, about our families, about our hopes, wishes, dreams, and concerns with each other via text.

The truth is, at that time, running kept me sane. There

were so many things taken from all of us during those many months. The calendar was basically empty. I experienced a lot of sadness, loneliness, and an antsy-ness brought on by a major case of cabin fever. For somebody like me, who is so detailed, so organized, so Type A, so calendar and plan driven, it felt like the rug was pulled out from under me. Yes, we were still homeschooling, so that really didn't change at all. As I previously mentioned, we were still able to go to physical therapy. But the rest of life HALTED. Our constantly on the go household was together all the time. I missed seeing friends. I missed the extra stuff the big kids were involved in. I missed the simple things: going to a playground, enjoying a movie, or meeting people for dinner or a game night. It felt in many ways as if life had stopped.

Some days I felt like I was reeling. With all that stuff stripped away, I quickly discovered that my "got it all together" exterior which has existed forever was a rather thinly veiled cover for some pretty serious anxiety. I needed control over something in my life and so many things were now out of my control entirely. I suddenly had some trouble making decisions, which had never been an issue before. I am nothing if not decisive. I became the queen of overthinking everything.

I had a couple of panic attacks at the store. Target has always been a "happy place" for me, and I enjoy shopping in general, grocery shopping included. However, the combination of all the changes that had occurred, the unknown timeline for how long life would be "different," coupled with having to wear a mask and not being able to breathe, wondering how "COVID afraid" the other shoppers were ("Is it OK if I put this box back on the shelf? I changed my mind." "Are they watching me manhandle the avocados to check for ripeness?") put me over the top a couple of times. Would I run into an acquaintance who was a heavy duty anti-masker?

I was just following the rules as I had my entire life. Go along to get along and all that. I didn't want to make waves. Did I want to wear a mask? No. Was I afraid at all? Really, no. Was I more afraid of getting stopped at the entrance of Meijer and told I needed to put on a mask? Absolutely, yes.

When some stores were loosening their restrictions and I decided it was OK to walk right on in without a mask, I still was super hesitant. I constantly assessed how many others were wearing one. I made eye contact with the greeter to see how they responded to my smile. I had my hand on the mask in my pocket in case I chickened out and decided I ought to put it on. I played a role in order to not stand out. Frankly, that's been the goal much of my life. Blend in, get along, don't cause trouble, don't bring attention to myself. I didn't know where that line was anymore. No matter what I did, SOMEONE didn't agree and I was truly afraid there would be some confrontation. And for me that would be the worst.

Those panic attacks showed up out of the blue. Never having had them before, I was caught completely off guard: the need to stop what I was doing immediately, the need to not make eye contact with anyone, the need to pull my mask down because I suddenly couldn't breathe. Sounds around me muffled a bit and a kind of tunnel vision settled in. I had a voice in my head saying, "I've got to go. I've got to go." I needed to get out of the store NOW. I left a cart two different times, half loaded with stuff, just because I couldn't be there anymore. I then sat in my car and cried. What was happening to me? I've got my act together. I've always had my act together. Or have I?

Another time a panic attack hit in the parking lot of Meijer and I didn't even go in. It felt like an enormously impossible task to go into the store and buy the groceries. This simple task I do on a weekly basis and have never had issue with, suddenly caused me great dismay. I had that same hyperfocused vision and a voice in my head repeating, "I can't go in. I can't go in."

I believed at the time there wasn't much I could do to control the "out of control" that I felt. Even seeking counseling, although perhaps one of the best things I could have done, didn't really feel like an option at the time. I wasn't interested in starting therapy via a ZOOM-style meeting. It felt like there would be such a lack of personal connection, especially since I wouldn't already have a relationship formed with the counselor.

So, I poured myself into the marathon training. I didn't miss a single workout. If the plan said I was to complete a 12-mile run, I didn't complete 11.97 miles, I completed the full 12. I ate well, having been mostly whole food plant-based for a couple of years already, and I read blogs and books and websites about properly fueling for endurance training.

I examined the weather and planned my day according to the real-feel temps. I timed my food around when I needed to run to fit it into the day—too close to the start time and I'd feel miserable, a run too late in the day and I'd have a headache from lack of food and not enough energy to complete the distance needed. I planned to make sure someone was home to keep my little guys occupied. When was sunset? Could I beat it? I found solace and peace through the physical movement. I listened to loud music with a driving beat. I alternately cried out to God with questions and sadness then praises of thanksgiving. I felt the big deep emotions about everything going on in my life. I wasn't just working through the losses that COVID presented. I was feeling the grief and loss surrounding my boys. I was mourning the future in many ways. I was looking for hope and comfort. Through the process of training for the marathon, there were days I was able to discover the calmest of calms.

As the weeks progressed and my scheduled runs became longer, I found that the "tired enough to take the edge off" really was helping me. My mind was clearer, my emotions were better in check, and I felt fantastic physically. Anne and I waited for word on whether we'd actually be able to run the marathon in Chicago or not.

When the announcement finally came that they would not be holding an in-person event, I was extremely disappointed. We both were. We didn't want to end the training because we'd already come so far. At the same time, we didn't really see the point in continually upping the mileage with no final event to culminate this process. The wheels started turning, what could we do instead? How can we make this training feel like it was worthwhile? We couldn't quit.

I brainstormed during a run the same afternoon we heard Chicago was a virtual-only option and came up with the rough elements of a plan. I knew who I could ask to help me organize an event. Phyllis, Carol, and Karen are amazing at that kind of thing! We would call it the Lemons to Lemonade 26.2, you know, because when life gives you lemons…Several additional weeks of planning brought this little idea to fruition.

We ran it the day before the Chicago Marathon was supposed to have happened, on a Saturday in October. It was held in the country near my home, on a route 6.55 miles long that we lapped 4 times, avoiding where I know dogs live, skirting around busy roads—with our friend, Liz, manning an aid station set up in the driveway of Steve and Phyllis's house. We turned the event into a fundraiser for the parsonage project which was already well underway, and we ended up raising nearly $7,500.

A small group of people met us for the 6 am start in the church parking lot. We had an actual starting gun! Two runners, 26.2 miles. Our friend, Jeff, rode his bike back and forth along the course to check on us. Erik and Karen drove laps in their Jeep to deliver more water and monitor our status. Each time we came up the last half mile stretch of the loop back north to the church parking lot, a slightly larger group of people was waiting to cheer us on.

There was a balloon arch for the finish line. We had a medal presentation, because of course we had to commemorate our first marathon in some tangible way (and I like the bling!). We sold Lemons to Lemonade T-shirts as part of the fundraising effort. A pizza truck was on-site serving lunch, and Frank's band performed on the lawn. Students from Ruth's dance studio performed several numbers as an additional part of the afternoon's entertainment. The weather was ideal. We literally could not have hoped for better. The number of people who came to observe, cheer, hang out, eat, be entertained, whatever the reason, was so amazing!

That longest, most difficult run of my life was part of one of the best days I've ever experienced. COVID was still heavy, and restrictions were in place nearly everywhere, but our event was held outdoors. We had so much love and support for this life changing (and I don't say that lightly) event. The day felt hopeful and charged with joy and accomplishment. It felt like a sneak peak into the return to normal life, something I had missed so desperately for months. It was wonderful to have such an event come together in a very short time. It was amazing to have the level of support we felt: in the planning stages, by the numbers in attendance, and through the financial contributions. It was fantastic to have accomplished this monumental goal side by side with one of my dearest friends.

But then it was done. I'll be honest (might as well be, I have been with everything else so far here), I felt lost again after the marathon was over. I had experienced the high of such a physical and mental accomplishment and then there wasn't another goal. Marathon wishful thinking turned into a plan turned into training had taken up a year.

What next now? I didn't have a milestone to reach toward. Then the weather turned because, well, winter. I was still running kind of consistently, trying not to let regular life get in the way, because I knew how good it was for both my physical and mental health. I borrowed a treadmill and set it up in the sun room of the rental we were in at the time. Then the treadmill went kaput. Too cold, too windy, too tired, too late in the day, too many things to get done, no one to stay with the boys...the list of excuses got longer and longer and longer.

So, I quit running. It was never an intentional decision, but life DID get in the way. The busyness of the schedule for the other big people in our house returned full steam ahead: school, work, dance, trainings, meetings, service planning, social engagements, and you name it. Carving out time in the day became difficult at best, and it was a chore that I eventually quit struggling to maintain. Anne and I signed up for the Chicago Marathon in both 2021 and 2022. Due to scheduling conflicts, injuries, and other life stuff, we didn't run either of those years, but were able to meet the fundraising commitment on behalf of PPMD.

Since then? I have settled into an overall peace for the most part, with purposeful living, trying to soak in the moments and memories with my family. I know how quickly time moves. I've experienced it firsthand with Gabriel and Kaleigh. A blink. That's it. A blink. Although certainly not every day or in every moment, I'm generally a more relaxed mama. I have a wee bit more patience for nonsense and childishness. I more greatly appreciate the cleverness and insight from my small boys. I am more generally content in my days and appreciative of my few very close friendships.

However, other things have suffered. I'm not taking as much time to prepare my own food separate from the rest of the household and allowing quite a bit of dairy and some meat back into my life. The result? My stomach protests on a daily basis. I know how to change it, fix it, but I haven't yet. The laser focus of fitness and training and exercise has also gone by the wayside. It has slowly maneuvered out of my daily plan so that it's really beyond even an afterthought. It's sometimes not even a shadow of a glimpse of an idea. The result? I'm more physically tired. I don't feel as strong and healthy. In the last 24 months I've gained almost 40 pounds, and I'm not comfortable with that. My clothes don't fit how I'd like them to and I do miss the leaner version of me from not too long ago.

How to find that balance then? I don't have aspirations to be as insanely fit as I was in the fall 2020—I'm not sure I could if I tried, especially without so much else having to slide at home or with my family, or my time and responsibilities as mom, teacher, wife and stay-at-home parent.

I DO know that I need to get a bit of a better handle on the amount and type of food I'm eating. I need to make the time to be able to more easily make the healthier choices I know have worked before and made me feel good. I DO know that I need some more physical activity. We now own another treadmill, so even a three mile walk in the evening after the boys are in bed, or an early morning walk before others get up would provide amazing benefits. I typically try to meet Karen once a week to go walk and catch up at a nearby forest preserve. Those days are amazing. However, I need to get more in on a daily basis so that my body is moving. I also greatly miss the yoga class I was previously going to one or two times each week.

I've let my physical self become less of a priority, and I want to get a bit of that back. Even a bit would be a big deal. And I would love to run again. I truly have zero aspirations to do another marathon, but working back up to half marathon distance would feel like an amazing accomplishment. I know it's doable. I just need to start the process over again. In fact, Anne and I took a leap of faith and are both registered for two half marathons in the spring. We are praying that good health and mental and physical commitment prevail.

The crazy of the schedule at the Estby household has returned to the pre-COVID norm. That alone has helped my mental health quite a bit. I'm able to again be "in charge" of the calendar. That brings me peace. The intention of purposeful living and awareness of being in the moment has also added significantly to my calm. I find great solace and respite when I sneak some time on the "coffee porch" (a small spot off the master bedroom). It's quiet and private. It's a safe spot where our dog can come sit with me without having to worry about her being leashed, and the boys know where to find me if they need something.

Truly, as I had hoped in the preface, this writing process HAS been amazingly therapeutic for me. I've enjoyed having a project to work on. I've relived so many memories. I've shed countless tears and worked through some big emotions. Grief is always with me. Anticipatory grief can be a beast.

Sometimes it's right in my face. At other times it serves merely as a background character. However, God's faithfulness in our lives and through our story has been brought front and center. Despite the very difficult things in life, I am reminded daily of His numerous blessings.

Ten

The Gift of Family

W e've been told so many times that we are a blessing to the boys, that they're lucky to have us, but WE are the ones who are lucky. I can't emphasize that enough. I fully realize we chose to bring them into our lives. We knew Samuel's diagnosis before we met him. We knew the chance of Josiah also having Duchenne when we agreed to adopt Samuel's sibling.

Most people don't invite this thing into their lives, but as I elaborated a bit before, I can honestly say we wouldn't have if Samuel had come to us sooner. We would have said "no, thank you." I know it. We would have taken a pass on this little guy with a terminal diagnosis. We would have protected ourselves from the scary reality of an "unhealthy child." We would also have missed out on two of the greatest blessings of our lives.

Most families have this unexpectedly thrust upon them. What a life-changing diagnosis. What a weight to carry. What a devastating turn in life's path. I really can't imagine how that experience plays out in one's mind and emotions.

But here's the truth of it: We answered God's call. We don't see ourselves as anything other than doing our best to be obedient. I believe Cory answered God's call when he left his job and we moved to the seminary for him to begin his pastoral training. I believe we answered God's call when we received word of this precious baby in need of a home, a call we would have ignored or rejected on an earlier timeline (on OUR timeline). And Josiah? He's a bonus blessing we never would have had opportunity to know if we hadn't again answered God's call. A choice? Maybe not so much. I described it before as a time "you can't possibly do anything other than say, 'yes, of course.'"

The boys are such a gift to us. They've taught us so many lessons and given us a second run at parenting in a different way. My big kids have turned out pretty well so far, but I was a much more unsure, short-tempered, and controlling parent with them, with nothing but immense love and a steep learning curve as the foundation for all of that. For better or worse, they survived and are thriving. These little guys have allowed our big kids to experience both the joys and irritations of having much younger siblings in the house, with bigger needs and more attention required at times, but also with so many of those snuggly hugs and sweet yet snarky comments and the budding wit and wisdom of elementary-aged kids.

I'm definitely more tired this go around. At this point, we've been parenting for almost 20 years. Samuel and Josiah are only 8 and 6, so we have so many more years to go. Despite the tired, or maybe due to it, I'm able to be a bit more introspective these days. I'm a wee bit more mellow and fully aware of the need to do my best to embrace every moment and take it all in for the time I have with them. Some days are HARD, really hard. I'm not gonna lie, some days seem downright miserable, but there are so many beautifully lovely moments mixed in.

My kids are pretty amazing, and just the right people I needed in my life. I thank God for entrusting their care to Cory and me:

Gabriel is a bit short-tempered at times like his mama, but has a ready laugh and an amazing sense of humor. He's mature, generous, so easygoing and likable, and a fantastic big brother. He's found his niche as a first responder and continues his training toward paramedic certification.

He has also found his own ways to accommodate his hearing loss through the years: continued lipreading, positioning in a classroom to better see faces and be less distracted, and asking for repetition. There is also a small group of people who know him well enough to realize when he doesn't hear an important part of a conversation (me, his girlfriend— Grace, Grace's parents—Steve and Constance, a couple of his coworkers at the fire station. We will repeat what was missed.) He also has a special stethoscope which pairs with his hearing aids through Bluetooth to transmit cardiac sounds directly to his aids. It's incredible, isn't it? Even 10 years ago, it would have been difficult or impossible for someone with a hearing loss as significant as his to be able to work as an EMT/paramedic. Despite his crazy busy work and school schedule, I'm so happy that he still lives close enough that we get to see him a couple of times a week. I'm incredibly proud of the young man he has become.

Kaleigh, at times, has been a bit moody (typical teen girl, right?), but she's also beautiful, talented, kind, and too modest to her own detriment. She loves her brothers (and our dog, Winnie) fiercely. She has the best smile. She's becoming more bold in finding her place in the world, is making good decisions and taking opportunities. This additional maturity is a wonderful thing to observe from afar. We miss her immensely, but are so proud of her step into college life and her choice to major in dance performance and choreography. We can't wait to see what the future holds for her.

Samuel can be bossy and a bit of a know-it-all, but he's also known as "The Professor" in a good way. He is both serious and wise. He has a sweet smile and a quick wit. I'm so entertained by how well he understands wordplay and humor. He's thoughtful, kind, and loves a good laugh. I love how he hums to himself throughout the day.

Josiah puts on a tough guy exterior, but way down deep he's the sweetest little thing. He's funny, interesting, and the most energetic and creative of our brood. He's very bright, prone to act a little crazy and a bit naughty, but he's also finding his way as the "baby" of the family, figuring out where and how he fits in. He still sneaks into our bed with regularity for snuggles and a warm body to rest against, and he asks for back scratches with his adorable little lisp. I love how he'll state something as a fact and then say, "Right, mommy?" to double check that his info is accurate. I appreciate that he trusts I won't lead him astray.

As much as Duchenne brings difficulty and dismay, there have been so many hidden blessings also given to us by its presence in our lives; the opportunity to meet so many other amazing Duchenne families, the knowledge gained and deep wonderful conversations we have with those interested in our "cause," the gift of so many people surrounding us with love and support in so many ways.

Another one that took me by surprise is this: You know those parenting moments that you never knew were the last? The last nap your child took on your chest, the last time they held your hand in a parking lot, or the transition when "mommy" becomes "mom"; I have the difficult blessing of feeling when the end might be coming for some of these physical skills and milestones of childhood.

I sit at a playground right now watching Samuel. It's more of a struggle today for him to climb up those couple of steps and get up from the base of the slide. Today, Josiah's gait seems a little more labored when running from one end of the park to the other. They are still so full of joy and the ability to play, but I see that our playground days are numbered. The ability to observe and know that there is a limited timeline does allow me to try to cement into my memories these moments before they are no longer.

As frustrated, tired, annoyed, irritated (fill in any other word you'd like) as I may be at times, Samuel and Josiah have brought immense JOY and LAUGHTER to our family and I can't imagine life without them as our sons. I am so very grateful for all of the roadblocks and struggles that were in the way along the way in order to get them to us according to God's plan. And I've learned so many lessons through all of that.

Eleven

Lessons for Navigating Grief

I 'm 46 years old. That's old enough to have a bit of a clue about life and people, and time enough to experience things that have taught me truths. It's also young enough that I'm not so naive to think I have it all figured out. I've learned important lessons about myself and about the people around me, but there are many more lessons I am working through right now. There are even so many more than that ahead for me, I know it. Experience and life's happenings teach us much and there are lessons to be learned in every circumstance: how to better react to a situation, how to treat others with more compassion and understanding, how your decisions not only affect you but everyone in your own little world, how to put your trust in God, not yourself…and many, many more.

Here are a few of the very important ones I've been able to take away from our life together so far:

1 - There is no shame or guilt in feeling how you feel.

It's OK to be sad—to cry in the middle of yoga class, or in your car. On the flip side, it's also OK to be happy. There is a lot of joy in life and peace to be found in the quiet moments. Embrace those moments with thankfulness because they might be few and far between at times.

I never really used to show what felt to me like "too much emotion." I was more than a little bit embarrassed to reveal what I believed to be weakness. Now I understand that's ridiculous. I've always been very honest, but truthfully, a little bit guarded. I didn't want to burden other people with my troubles, which is also ridiculous. It has taken a very long time to move through that feeling. I do feel things deeply, and I'm a little more likely now to share it, to show it, but I still have a long way to go. Emotion is not a sign of weakness, it's a sign of humanity. I'm not a robot affected by nothing, moving through the day without flinching. My feelings get hurt. I love fiercely. I overthink and am anxious about things. I feel great pride and joy in the amazing young adults my older children have become. However, I'm still very private.

I know a few people who have had traumatic life-changing experiences. Unbelievable and unspeakable loss and pain has changed them. They seem, at least from the outside, to feel little joy, to have a sorrow embedded in their soul that they can't shake. I pray that even in my most difficult days I will be able to find some joy and peace and that the Lord would provide me with comfort. I also pray that I will be able to cry when I need to cry and grieve when I need to grieve, and not be afraid to let others see it.

2 - Take/make/protect time for yourself.

Maybe it's a mani/pedi (not my kind of thing, but you know...), going for a run, window shopping, coffee with a friend, socializing or being alone, music and meditation, prayer, journaling, or reading your Bible. Self-care is the buzz word. I don't care for that moniker, but I suppose it does get the point across. We all need some carved out time alone, or instead, doing something we love with someone else if that's more your style. Finding something for YOU is so important to your spirit. Your loved one needs you, but they need you at your best—or at least as your decently adequate self. If you're not sleeping well, feeling run down, or completely preoccupied with your loved one's medical or physical care, you will not be able to serve them well.

Feeling selfish or guilty can disrupt these opportunities. I've felt that. I've gone for one of those really long marathon training runs, fully expecting it to take three and a half to four hours. Others in the household had to rearrange or delay their schedule so I could fit it in. As mom, as primary caregiver, as the stay-at-home parent, as the homeschool teacher, I so often feel obligated to be here and available all the time.

There are other times when I don't feel that huge tug to have to be present, but once out and doing something fun, interesting, or just for me, I have often ended up with a tinge of selfishness that I'm enjoying myself or guilt that somebody might need something. I'm slowly getting better about that, knowing that the boys (and the household) are left in capable enough hands—whether it's my husband, the big kids, or a sitter. I know things can be dealt with appropriately by them or wait until I return home.

I am also realizing it is good for the boys to spend time with other people and apart from me. It is good for me to spend time apart from them. Interactions are a little smoother, and I find we are all a little less irritable after we've had some time apart, especially after long stretches of so much time together.

I love the opportunity to participate weekly in a book/dinner club hosted locally, grab coffee and catch up with a friend, go out to dinner or on a road trip with some other couples we love to spend time with, or just invite people over for a game night.

3 - Learn what you can.

I said it earlier, knowledge is power. Join Facebook groups with people facing the same diagnosis. Seek out organizations who serve through advocacy and education. Reach out to other families or support groups to potentially compare notes and offer mutual care and concern. Find out what to expect down the road. There may be things that can help slow progress or increase comfort. Attend conferences or workshops if at a feasible cost or reasonable distance. Gather up-to-date information on the standards of care and the newest treatment protocols available. Decide if your family is interested in pursuing clinical trials.

All of the above are amazing opportunities for you to learn more about the needs your loved one has and to better prepare you to ask questions and advocate. However, don't obsess. Don't fret about not doing enough. Make an honest effort and love your loved one. Serve them well. That's the most important piece. Be educated and prepared. The truth is, there may come a time when you sit back and let things just happen. There is no harm in that either, because the time may come when quality of life is of prime importance, when making memories and experiencing joy will take priority.

4 - Don't be afraid to reach out for help.

Consider counseling, share your fears and concerns with friends, secure respite care if needed. I've not yet sought counseling, but I do believe it can serve a real purpose and will probably be a necessity for me at some point. Right now the boys are young enough and in good enough physical condition that day-to-day stuff is pretty "normal."

I have a group of friends who offer an outlet for care and support via daily text messages and occasional dinners out. Those "cactus" friends (we joke that we're a group of people who aren't typically huggers, although we do hug each other!) have become so very dear to me. For now, they are all the therapy I need. We commiserate, console, and support. We cry and we laugh—so much laughter! The friendships with these women bring a comfort to my spirit.

Today I'm doing OK with all the stuff—school and PT and playtime and little adventures. This is mostly normal parenting, outside of the OCD/sensory piece, but even that is not uncommon. Our everyday feels pretty typical to me, or at least it's our typical.

Mixed in with the humdrum are many bittersweet moments. Watching Samuel sit and rest at a playground makes me sad for him, although he seems content to watch. Seeing both boys run across the yard, noticing how Samuel can't keep up with his younger brother, breaks me a little. Josiah talks about wanting to be a farmer or a firefighter like his big brother, Gabriel, when he grows up. The boys talk about moving out when they're adults. They joke about what they'll be like when they're "old bald grandpas." They want to have lots of pets when out and living on their own.

Maybe none of this is impossible, but it will be complicated, difficult, and somewhat unlikely. I am aware of some young men with Duchenne who go to college, have full-time personal care assistants, and live semi-independently in an apartment. So many of them don't get that chance. Many die young and don't have the opportunity to experience so much of life that most of us typically take for granted.

The stark truth and likely reality is that my sons probably won't learn how to drive a car, and they are much less likely to get married and have children (although a handful of men with Duchenne do just that). They are probably with us in our home until they lose their battle with Duchenne.

I know difficult days are ahead as their daily care becomes more physically demanding on both my husband and me as caregivers. As Duchenne robs more and more from them, I know that I'll feel the true enormity of this diagnosis and how it will eventually become a part of every aspect of our lives. I know that counseling for me, for my husband, for us as a couple, for our older children, and for the boys as they're experiencing these changes and losses and require more dependence on us, will likely be necessary.

5 - Take care of yourself physically.

Your loved one relies on you to be healthy and strong, or as strong as you can be. By keeping physically fit, I hope to be better able to transfer from bed to wheelchair or wheelchair to toilet as time goes along. Equipment (Hoyer lift, shower chair) helps, but there is still a physical component to the care. The longer I can stay healthy and strong the less likely I will end up potentially being forced to rely on outside help for the boys. I hope to be around for them as long as they need me.

How do I accomplish that? I need to exercise regularly, whether it's taking a brisk walk, running, biking, swimming, or even simply trying for constant movement throughout the day. I need to eat healthy food. I know what foods make me feel amazing and what foods make me feel sluggish and slow. I know which foods will bother my stomach. It's a matter of making choices I know in my head will make me FEEL better vs. the salty or sweet foods that sounds so delicious. I'm a sucker for pizza, mashed potatoes, mac 'n' cheese, fried chicken and nachos—all of which make my tummy protest.

Keep regular medical and dental appointments. Don't delay when you're truly ill or need to get something checked out. I'm super guilty of waiting and assuming things will "get better" - i.e., the two and half month sinus infection that "will eventually go away."—it did, but I was miserable for weeks. Being in my best health means the boys get the best care I can give them.

6 - Seek a support network.

Find support in your immediate and extended family, neighbors, fellow churchgoers, friends already in your "circle," or others with the same diagnosis who might be either ahead, beside, or behind you in this journey, in person or via social media groups.

My husband's position as a pastor moved us far from family long ago. We see relatives rather infrequently, so have made a home and a family with those around us. We have had a number of adopted grandparents for our children since the big kids were little. We have many supportive acquaintances, friends of a friend, and an extended family of friends and church members. We have a smaller group of close friends so dear to us that they are indeed family to us. We share in each other's joys and burdens. We are raising children and grandchildren together. We pray for and support each other daily. We are blessed to have all of these people in our lives.

I've joined several Facebook groups specifically for Duchenne families: a general DMD group, one specifically for kids under 10, one for housing modifications and accessible transportation info, and one for parents of older boys and young men. I purposefully turned off notifications for the general and older boys group, because I was having a hard time reading some of the posts. Although totally relevant, supportive, and likely helpful for the families in those stages, I found it to be overwhelming for me at this point. The daily struggles, the sadness, and sometimes the anger at God, brought me down. We're not at that stage, and while I fully believe in having a realistic understanding of expectations for the future, I'm not prepared to have that right in front of me all the time. I intend to certainly rejoin those groups when we're at that point.

I have found the groups appropriate to our current age/stage/need are fantastic:

-I learned that a standard minivan base is not strong enough to hold two power chairs and that we will be better served when the time comes to purchase something like a Ford Transit.

-At Kohl's, of all places, I found an adaptive style bicycle for Samuel that is available for less than $300 (Specialized companies offer them for $1,500-$3,000+). He should be able to use for at least a couple of years. I was able to share that information with some of these groups and later learned others had taken my suggestion and purchased one themselves.

-I discovered transitioning from a medical stroller to a wheelchair may serve your child best, OR transitioning to a scooter of sorts may be a better choice in the interim at a lower cost.

-I learned that pediatric sized medical scooters do not exist. Adult sized scooters can be adapted by cutting down a post, building up a footrest, and/or adding backrest support.

-I learned that medical insurance may not cover both a medical scooter and a power chair if the need arises sooner than expected and a certain period of time has not yet passed. These are bits of information I'm certain I wouldn't easily be able to gain anywhere else. What a wealth of information!

Through the workshops and different events we've attended, Cory and I have been able to meet two other families in our general area with boys with Duchenne. Both are older than our sons by several years, but because of our similar circumstances, we've been able to connect and offer support to one another. We have occasional conversations via text, visit during dinner at each other's houses, and meet for coffee. I call my friend, Kim, my Duchenne mommy mentor. I don't know if that's a title she embraces, but I'm so thankful that we've become friends. Putting aside the Duchenne diagnosis, I just really like her. It's so nice to know that we aren't alone, and a reassurance to them in the same regard, I hope.

7 - Have a willingness to be open and transparent about your life: your struggles, fears, triumphs.

This allows connections with others. Vulnerability can be so hard, but it's necessary. This lesson has been crucial for me to learn over the last several years. This can help someone with their pain—it can also help you with yours. Mutual support can be offered. It can be really nice to know you're not alone.

Everyone you know is going through something. Secrets and sadness lead to walls being built up and tear down relationships. I have zero training in counseling or psychology, but I know that in the relationships and friendships I am the most open, I also receive the most reward, comfort, and consolation. A level of trust is built and that in itself can offer immense peace. Those friendships bring much joy to my spirit, despite what a particular day may hold. Sharing in joys, in addition to those struggles, allows a happy energy to be built and positive feelings to exist. These can help you through the most difficult days.

8 - Try not to be weighed down by the day-to-day.

Physical and medical needs can become overwhelming because they are ever present. Seek out opportunities and experiences for yourself (see #2 above) and for your family as a whole. What does your loved one enjoy? Where do they want to go? What shared experiences would you like to have with them? Check things off of a bucket list or make simple outings a joy and a pleasure, as long as it's together and doing something they love or seeing something of beauty. Accommodations may be needed for travel and explorations, but creativity can help with this! Life isn't "normal" in so many ways when dealing with medical and physical needs, but you can find things which feel more normal and bring joy and excitement, providing something to look forward to.

9 - Don't parent a child differently just because of a diagnosis.

I heard of a family who had zero expectations for their son with Duchenne to participate in the running of the household in any way, even though at that point he was rather young and certainly physically able to do many things (help with laundry, make his own bed, set the table for dinner, or carry his plate to the sink. So many simple chores!). Similarly, I have read social media posts about a mom who was afraid to discipline her young son despite some deplorable behavior and foul words being spit out at her. She felt sorry for him and his "curse of a disease." She was miserable, her son had no friends, and she felt her life was falling apart. His behaviors were only a piece of the puzzle, but a bit of discipline/change of course in parenting and the expectations for her son certainly couldn't have hurt.

Of course, you must take into consideration any physical limitations, learning styles, and the emotional struggles. We involve our sons in household activities and chores as it seems appropriate. We encourage them to participate in the ways they can as part of our family, looking toward adaptations and accommodations as needed.

Inappropriate behavior is still inappropriate behavior. We offer grace in relation to their limitations, but keep in mind uncorrected negative behavior will continue or get worse. There still should be consequences for actions. A reward system and time outs may look a little different. Discipline is necessary to teach social interactions and rule following for school and home interactions—and to turn out decent human beings who people actually want to be around.

10 - Find a place that's yours.

This might be a rocker on the porch, a spot at your favorite coffee shop, or a quiet corner of your house. In a pinch, sitting in your car or even in the bathroom with the door closed could work. Find a place where you can take a moment when you're overwhelmed—a place of solitude and quiet where you can think, meditate, or pray for a few moments by yourself, on a daily basis, or on an as-you-need-it basis.

My spot is the front porch of our house. I've spoken about it before. The "coffee porch" is a quiet little nook added by the architect during the design phase and it's perfect. It faces the road, so if I want to people watch or just sit and gaze at the field of corn across the road, I can. There's enough of an overhang that it's well protected from most of the wind we get (so much wind!!!) and much precipitation. There's a railing all the way around, so it's kind of blocked off from visitors showing up at that end of the house. It only has access through the master bedroom, so it's definitely private. With a couple of rockers, a small table, a little solar lamp and string lights hung, I have a mini-oasis.

I truthfully don't know that in the time we've lived in this home that my husband has been out here other than to show it as part of a tour when someone comes over. I say "out here," because that's where I'm sitting right now, typing. This is where 85% of this has been written. I know the boys are safe, watching TV, playing on their iPads, or running in the yard right here in front of me when the weather is agreeable. This is my safe place. I can read, write, zone out, or pray. Even a 15 minute snippet of time can bring me some peace. Sometimes, I'm out here an hour.

Other times I'm able to have some time in the hot tub by myself after the boys are in bed. It's super fun to have friends over to enjoy some conversation and drinks, but it's also an amazing place to just relax and enjoy the quiet. I play soft music through the speakers and close my eyes while enjoying the warmth. The hot tub has definitely become a second "happy place" for me.

11 - Cling to your faith.

God is ever present, whether you feel Him right beside you or not. I know not everyone is a Christian. I realize that not everyone holds to a belief system. I do. I was raised in the church. I attended parochial school from four-year-old preschool through high school. My husband is a pastor, and the church is a big part of our weekly/daily experience. I'm surrounded by such a large number of kind, generous, faithful people with the love of Christ in their hearts which shines forth in their love for others.

I have been the recipient of so much of that love and blessed by beautiful friendships with women I know I can trust and who support one other. I have felt the humility that comes after such generosity that I can't find words to speak the gratitude in my spirit. At my lowest, I cry out to Him. At my most triumphant, I try not to take the good for granted, but to instead sing His praises and give thanks.

Twelve

What Next?

We know Duchenne is a death sentence. However, we don't know when the end will be. The truth is, we don't know when the end will be for any of us. Our family made a purposeful decision to not focus on the grief and sadness. Will we be sad? Are there days and seasons during which we will struggle? Of course there will be.

However, we choose daily to live to the best of our ability. Life is not about living with anticipation of grief. It's about living together in grace and joy. It's about loving the people around us through each of the moments we have on earth together.

Cory and I have experienced so much together. At this point we've known each other for 28 years and have been married for 23. He has been a rock and faithful partner to me, and I hope that I've been able to support him as best I can. We are trying to raise our children with the knowledge that they are loved immensely—by us, of course, but also by those who surround our family with love, compassion, generosity, and care. They also know how much they are loved by God. I pray for peace, love, joy, and comfort through all of our days.

There's so much of our story to come.

Made in the USA
Coppell, TX
18 December 2022